Academic Writing

A practical guide for students

Stephen Bailey

Text © Stephen Bailey 2003
Original illustrations © Nelson Thornes Ltd 2003

Published in 2003 by:
Nelson Thornes Ltd
Delta Place
27 Bath Road
Cheltenham
GL53 7TH
United Kingdom

03 04 05 06 07 / 10 9 8 7 6 5 4 3 2 1

A catalogue record for this book is available from the British Library.

ISBN 0 7487 6838 6

Illustrations by Oxford Designers and Illustrators
Page make-up by Northern Phototypesetting Co. Ltd, Bolton

Printed and bound in Great Britain by Ashford Colour Press

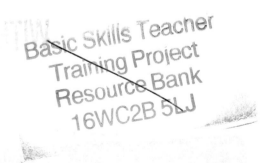

Acknowledgements

I would like to thank the staff and students at the Centre for English Language Education (CELE) at The University of Nottingham who have piloted these materials, and in particular my colleagues Ann Smith, Janet Sanders and Sandra Haywood for their specific contributions in unravelling some of the finer points of academic language. My wife, Rene, deserves my warmest thanks for her unfailing support, advice and encouragement over the whole period of the project's development.

The author and publishers wish to thank the following for permission to reproduce photographs and other copyright material in this book.

Corel 76 (NT) p 29; Corel 102 (NT) p 90; Corel 392 (NT) p 118; Corel 631 (NT) p33; Corel 786 (NT) p 19; Corel 787 (NT) p 41; Joe Cornish/Digital Vision LL (NT) p 38; Illustrated London News V1 (NT) p 56; Illustrated London News V2 (NT) p 4; Photodisc 31 (NT) p 78 ; Photodisc 41 (NT) p 46; Photodisc 46 (NT) pp 56, 80; Photodisc 71 (NT) p 8; Photodisc 72 (NT) p 17; Stockbyte 31 (NT) p 60.

Every effort has been made to contact copyright holders and the publishers apologise to anyone whose rights have been inadvertently overlooked and will be happy to recitfy any errors or omissions.

Contents

Introduction

Academic Writing is designed for anybody who is studying (or planning to study) at English-medium colleges and universities and has to write essays and other assignments for exams or coursework. International students especially find the written demands of their courses extremely challenging. On top of the complexity of the vocabulary of academic English they have to learn a series of conventions in style, referencing and organisation.

Academic Writing is a flexible course that allows students to work either with a teacher or by themselves, to practise those areas which are most important for their studies. Many students find that they have very limited time to prepare for their courses, and that writing is only one of several skills they need to master. The structure of the book has been made as simple as possible to allow users to find what they want quickly.

The course is organised to provide maximum hands-on practice for students. Skills are developed from writing at the paragraph level, through organising the various sections of an essay, to discussing statistics and describing charts. This book is divided into four parts:

1) *The Writing Process* guides students from the initial stage of understanding an essay title, through reading and note-making, to the organisation of an essay and the final stage of proof-reading.

2) *Elements of Writing* deals with the key skills that are needed for all types of assignments, such as making definitions and giving references, and is organised alphabetically.

3) *Accuracy in Writing* gives remedial practice in those areas that students tend to find most confusing, such as definite articles and relative pronouns, again in alphabetical order.

4) *Writing Models* gives examples of the types of writing that students commonly need, including letters and survey reports.

All units are cross-referenced and a comprehensive key is provided at the end. There is also a *Writing Tests* section for assessing level and progress.

Although every effort has been made to make *Academic Writing* as useful and accurate as possible, if students or teachers have any comments, criticisms or suggestions I would be very pleased to hear from them.

Stephen Bailey
academicwriting@beeb.net

Instructions to students are printed like this:
> *Complete the sentences with suitable words from the box below.*

Cross-references in margins look like this:

> **cross reference**
>
> *2.11 Synonyms*

This means: refer to the unit on synonyms in Part 2 (Unit 11).

1. The Writing Process

Student Introduction

Most academic courses in English-medium colleges and universities use essays to assess students' work, both as coursework, for which a deadline one or two months ahead may be given, and in exams, when an essay often has to be completed in an hour.

The process of writing essays for coursework assignments can be shown in a flowchart:

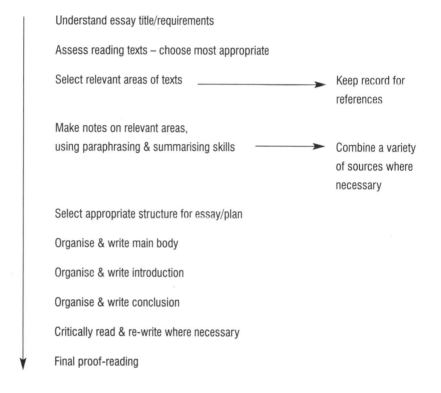

Understand essay title/requirements

Assess reading texts – choose most appropriate

Select relevant areas of texts ⟶ Keep record for references

Make notes on relevant areas, using paraphrasing & summarising skills ⟶ Combine a variety of sources where necessary

Select appropriate structure for essay/plan

Organise & write main body

Organise & write introduction

Organise & write conclusion

Critically read & re-write where necessary

Final proof-reading

Part 1, *The Writing Process*, examines each of these stages in turn. If students are concerned only with preparing for exam writing they could omit the reading and note-making stages, but if they have sufficient time they should work through every unit, preferably in the order given, for each stage builds on the previous one.

Although it is essential to understand the basic writing process, at the same time it will be useful to be aware of the elements which contribute to good academic writing. When practising note-making, for example, it is helpful to be aware of the conventions of referencing, and so students should use the cross-reference boxes to look at the unit on *References and Quotations* in Part 2.

1.   Background to Writing

Some of the terms used to describe different types of writing assignments can be confusing. In addition, students need to be clear about the basic components of written texts. This unit provides an introduction to these topics.

1. **Students may have to produce various types of written work as part of their courses.**

   Complete the table to show the main purpose of the following, and their usual approximate length.

Type	Purpose	Length
letter	for formal and informal communication	usually less than 500 words
notes		
report		
project		
essay		
thesis/dissertation		
article/paper		

2. **Organisation of texts.**

   a) *Explain the following terms in italic:*

   Shorter texts, e.g. essays, are normally organised in the form:

   Introduction > Main Body > Conclusion

   Longer texts, e.g. dissertations and articles, may include (depending on subject area):

   Abstract > Contents > Introduction > Main Body > Case Study > Discussion > Findings > Conclusion > Acknowledgements > Bibliography/References > Appendices

   Books may also contain:

   Dedication > Foreword > Preface > Index

   b) *Match the definitions below to one of the terms in (2a).*

   i)   Short summary (100–200 words) of the writer's purpose and findings   (.......)

   ii) Section where various people who assisted the writer are thanked   (.......)

   iii) Final part where extra data, too detailed for the main text, are stored   (.......)

   iv) List of all the books that the writer has consulted   (.......)

   v)   Section looking at a particular example relevant to the main topic   (.......)

   vi) Introductory part of book which may give the writer's motives   (.......)

   vii) Alphabetical list of all topics in the text   (.......)

3. Other text features.

Abbreviations are often used to save space:

Call Centres (CCs) feature prominently in the technology mix.

Italic is used to show titles and words from other languages:

Where once the titles of *Armchair Theatre* and *The Wednesday Play* celebrated …

Squatter housing (called *gecekondu* in Turkish) …

Footnotes are used to indicate references at the bottom of the page:

In respect of Singapore the consensus is that the government has made a difference.[3]

Endnotes are given to show references at the end of the article or chapter:

The market for masonry construction may be divided into housing and non-housing sectors [1]

Quotation marks are used to draw attention to a phrase, perhaps because it is being used in an unusual or new way:

The research shows that the 'pains of imprisonment' for women are…

4. All types of writing consist of a number of key elements.

Label the items in the text.

a) ……………… THE ORIGINS OF THE INDUSTRIAL REVOLUTION

b) ……………… Introduction

c) ……………… *It is generally agreed* that the Industrial Revolution began in Britain during the eighteenth century, with significant developments in the iron, steel and textile industries. But it is less clear what caused this sudden increase in production in key areas; different writers have examined the availability of capital, the growth of urban populations and the political and

d) .... religious climate. *All of these may have played a part, but first it is necessary to consider the precise nature of what is meant by 'Industrial Revolution'.*

e) .... *Industry had existed for thousands of years prior to the eighteenth century, but before this time society as a whole remained agricultural. With the arrival of the ironworks and cotton mills whole towns were dominated by industrial activity. At the same time, agriculture itself went through significant changes which produced more food for the growing urban population.*

cross reference

1.11   *Organising Paragraphs*
1.12   *Organising the Main Body*

5. **Why are all texts divided into paragraphs? How long are paragraphs?**
Read the following text, from the introduction to an essay, and divide it into a suitable number of paragraphs.

INVESTMENT

Most people want to invest for the future, to cover unexpected financial difficulties and provide them with security. Different people, however, tend to have different requirements, so that a 25-year-old just leaving university would be investing for the long-term, whereas a 60-year-old who had just retired would probably invest for income. Despite these differences, certain principles apply in most cases. The first issue to consider is risk. In general, the greater the degree of risk in investment, the higher the return. Shares, for example, which can quickly rise or fall in value, typically have a higher yield than bonds, which offer good security but pay only about 5% Therefore all investors must decide how much risk is appropriate in their particular situation. Diversification must also be considered in an investment strategy. Wise investors usually seek to spread their investments across a variety of geographical and business sectors. As accurate predictions of the future are almost impossible, it is best to have as many options as possible. A further consideration is investor involvement. Some investors opt for a high degree of involvement and want to buy and sell regularly, constantly watching the markets. Others want to invest and then forget about it. Personal involvement can be time-consuming and worrying, and many prefer to leave the management of their portfolios to professional fund managers.

2.   Developing Plans from Titles

Most written work begins with a title, and students must be quite clear what question the title is asking before starting to plan the essay and read around the topic. This unit deals with analysing titles and making basic plans.

1. **When preparing to write an essay, it is essential to identify the main requirements of the title. You must be clear about what areas your teacher wants you to cover. This will then determine the organisation of the essay. For example:**

   Academic qualifications are of little practical benefit in the real world – Discuss.

   Here the key word is *discuss*. Discussing involves examining the benefits and drawbacks of something.

   Underline the key words in the following titles and consider what they are asking you to do.

   a) Define Information Technology (IT) and outline its main applications in medicine.

   b) Compare and contrast the appeal process in the legal systems of Britain and the USA.

   c) Evaluate the effect of mergers in the motor industry in the last ten years.

   d) Trace the development of primary education in Britain. Illustrate some of the issues currently facing this sector.

   Note that most of the titles above have *two* terms in the title. You must decide how much importance to give to each section of the essay (e.g. title (a) might demand 10% for the definition and 90% for the outline).

2. **The following terms are also commonly used in essay titles.**

   Match the terms to the definitions on the right.

   Analyse   Give a clear and simple account

   Describe   Make a proposal and support it

   Examine   Deal with a complex subject by giving the main points

   State   Divide into sections and discuss each critically

   Suggest   Give a detailed account

   Summarise   Look at the various parts and their relationships

cross reference

1.10   Planning a Text
2.5   Discussion

3. **Almost all essays, reports and articles have the same basic pattern of organisation:**

Introduction
Main body
Conclusion

   The structure of the main body depends on what the title is asking you to do. In the case of a **discuss** type essay, the main body is often divided into two parts, one looking at the advantages of the topic and the other looking at the disadvantages.

   A plan for the first example might look like this:

Academic qualifications are of little practical benefit in the real world – Discuss.

Introduction	variety of different qualifications
	different methods of assessment
Benefits	international standards for professions, e.g. doctors
	students have chance to study latest theories
	qualifications lead to better salaries and promotion
Drawbacks	many successful people don't have qualifications
	many qualified people don't have jobs
Conclusion	qualifications are useful but not guarantees of success

4. *Write a plan for one of the titles in (1).*

title	
introduction	
main body	
conclusion	

5. **Teachers often complain that students write essays that do not answer the question set.**

   Consider the following titles and decide which sections should be included in each essay.

   a) Describe the growth of the European Union since 1975 and suggest its likely form by 2010.
      A short account of European history 1900–2000
      An analysis of candidates for membership before 2010
      A discussion of the current economic situation in Europe
      An outline of the enlargement of the EU between 1975 and now

   b) Summarise the arguments in favour of privatisation and evaluate its record in Britain.
      A case study of electricity privatisation
      An analysis of less successful privatisations
      A study of major privatisations in the UK
      A discussion of the benefits achieved by privatisation

   c) To what extent is tuberculosis (TB) a disease of poverty?
      A definition of TB

A report on the spread of TB worldwide

A case study showing how TB relates to social class

A discussion of new methods of treating the disease

d) Nursery education is better for children than staying at home with mother – Discuss.

A study of the growth of nurseries since 1995

A report on the development of children who remain at home until five

A discussion comparing speaking ability in the two groups of children

An outline of the increase of women in the labour market since 1960

e) Compare studying in a library with using the internet. Will the former become redundant?

The benefits of using books

The drawbacks of internet sources

Predicted IT developments in the next 15 years

An outline of developments in library services since 1945

6. *Underline the key terms in the following titles and decide what you are being asked to do.*

Example:

Relate the development of railways to the rise of nineteenth-century European nationalism.

Relate means to link one thing to another. The title is asking for links to be made between the growth of railways in Europe in the nineteenth century and the political philosophy of nationalism. The writer must decide if there was a connection or not.

a) Identify the main causes of rural poverty in China.

b) Calculate the likely change in coffee consumption that would result from a 10% fall in the price of coffee beans.

c) Classify the desert regions of Asia and suggest possible approaches to halting their spread.

3. Evaluating a Text

Having understood the title and made an outline plan, your next step is probably to read around the subject. Although you may be given a reading list, it is still vital to be able to assess the usefulness of journal articles and books. Time spent learning these skills will be repaid by saving you from using unreliable or irrelevant materials.

1. **When reading a text, it is important to ask yourself questions about the value of the text. Is this text fact or opinion? If fact, is it true? If opinion, do I agree? Can this writer be trusted? These questions can be shown in a diagram:**

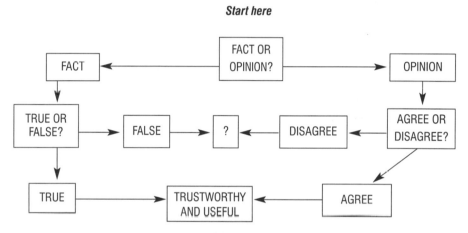

2. *Read the following sentences and decide first if they are fact or opinion. Then decide if the factual sentences are true, and if you agree with the opinions in the other sentences.*

		Opinion or fact?	Agree or disagree?	True or false?
a)	The USA has the biggest economy in the world			
b)	Shakespeare wrote textbooks			
c)	Shakespeare was a great writer			
d)	Smoking can be dangerous			
e)	Too many people (32%) smoke in Britain			
f)	95% of criminals cannot read			
g)	Poor education causes 75% of crime			

3. **It can be seen that even short sentences can contain a mixture of fact and opinion. Most longer texts, of course, consist of both.**

   Read the following and underline facts (____) and opinions (〜〜〜).

   a) Britain has one of the highest crime rates in the world.

   b) A robbery takes place every five seconds. A car is stolen every minute. Clearly, criminals are not afraid of the police.

   c) Even if they are caught, few criminals ever appear in court.

   d) Most of those who are found guilty are let off with a tiny fine.

   e) To restore law and order, we need many more police and much tougher punishments.

4. **The previous sentences can be evaluated as follows:**

   a) Fact, but only partly true. Britain does not have one of the highest overall crime rates in the world. For some crimes, e.g. car crime, the rate is high, but other countries, e.g. South Africa and the USA, have much higher rates of violent crime.

   b) These facts may or may not be true, but it is not clear from them that criminals are unafraid of the police.

   c) Fact, but not true. A significant number of those arrested are charged and later prosecuted.

   d) This statement is vague. A fine is not *letting off*. What is meant by *tiny*?

   e) This is a half-truth. More police would probably help reduce crime, but it is not clear if stronger punishments would have that result.

   From this it can be seen that even if the facts are correct, the opinions that are expressed may not be reliable. The evaluation above would suggest that the writer of the original text could not be trusted, and it would be better to look for another source.

5. *Evaluate the following passages in a similar way. First underline facts and opinion, then decide if the text as a whole is trustworthy.*

   a) Every year large numbers of students travel abroad to study at university. Most of them spend thousands of pounds on their degree courses. The cost of travel and accommodation adds significantly to their expenses. But they could save a lot of money by studying their courses online, using the internet and email. Increasing numbers of universities are offering tuition by the internet, and this has many advantages for students. In the future most students are likely to stay at home and study in front of a computer.

   b) London is an ideal city for young students. Britain's lively capital, with a population of two million, is the perfect place to live and study. Cheap, comfortable accommodation is always available, and transport is provided by the clean and reliable underground system. Another advantage is the friendly citizens, who are well-known for their custom of stopping to chat with strangers. Overall, London is probably the best place in the world to study English.

c) A leading academic has claimed that European unemployment has been made worse by high rates of home ownership. He argues that the growing trend towards owner-occupation is the best explanation for the high rates of unemployment in Europe. This, he argues, is because home owning makes people more reluctant to move if they lose their job. His research suggests that a strong private rented sector is the key to low unemployment. For example, Ireland, where only 9% rent their homes, has an unemployment rate of 8%. At the other extreme, Switzerland has a rental rate of 60%, but only 3% are unemployed.

d) Global warming affects most people in the world, especially those living in low-lying areas near the sea. It has been predicted that the melting of polar ice may cause the sea to rise by as much as twelve metres by 2050. This would cause flooding in many major coastal cities, such as Tokyo. It has been suggested that the best solution to this problem may be for mankind to become amphibious, like frogs. It is argued that life was originally found in the sea, and so it would merely be a return to our original habitat.

e) There is shocking new evidence of the effects of heavy alcohol consumption by young people. In Britain in 2000 nearly 800 people under 44 died from cirrhosis of the liver, a condition which is mainly caused by excess drinking. This is over four times higher than the number in 1970. As a result, the government is studying the possibility of compulsory health warnings on alcohol advertising. The growing problem seems to be due to 'binge' drinking among the young, when drinkers deliberately set out to get drunk.

4.   Understanding Purpose and Register

Having decided that a text is reliable, a student must read and understand as much as necessary for the needs of the essay. Understanding a text is not just a matter of vocabulary; the reader needs to find out the writer's intentions. Is the writer aiming to inform, persuade, describe or entertain? The answer to this question may affect the way a student uses the material.

1. *Compare the two extracts below:*

   a)   Rebus College is seeking candidates for the position of Treasurer. As the Chief Financial Officer of the College, the Treasurer is responsible for working with the senior administration and Trustees to develop and implement a financial strategic vision for the College.

   b)   Are you wondering what to do with that jumper you were given for Christmas that's two sizes too small – or worse, the personal stereo that simply doesn't work? Well, don't worry. Chances are, you'll be able to get your dud gifts swapped, fixed or get a refund. And, armed with our guide to your rights, you'll be able to get any defective products sorted.

   The first extract is written to **inform** the reader about a job vacancy and to give information about the work. The second aims to **persuade** the reader to buy the guide described. The language style, or register, of the extracts is also very different. The first uses very formal vocabulary such as *seeking*, *position* and *implement*. The second uses an informal tone, the pronoun *you*, the question form and informal vocabulary such as *dud* and *swapped*.

2. *Read the following extracts and complete the table using one or two of the following:* **inform/amuse/persuade/entertain.**

Text	Purpose
a	
b	
c	

   a)   The lower you are in the office hierarchy, the more disgusting your sandwiches. You can safely assume that a chicken and banana man is not a main board director. Some people, generally those in accounts, have had the same sandwich for the past 30 years. People like to prove how busy they are by eating their sandwich at their desk. But this is counter-productive, because every time you take a mouthful the phone rings, and you'll only get to finish that last mouthful just before you go home.

   b)   Writing for publication can be both profitable and enjoyable. It's open to everyone, because you don't need any qualifications. In Britain there is a huge demand for new materials, with thousands of newspapers and magazines published every week. In addition there are TV and radio programmes, the theatre and films. Given this situation, there are many openings for new writers. But the director of one of the UK's main writing colleges, the Writing Academy, advises: 'to enter this market successfully you must have good training'.

c)   The Advertising Standards Authority makes sure that advertising is legal, decent, honest and truthful. The Authority safeguards the public by ensuring that the rules contained in the British Code of Advertising Practice are followed by everyone who prepares and publishes advertisements in the UK, and that advice is freely available to prevent problems arising. The Code lays down what is and is not acceptable in advertisements, except for those on TV and radio.

3. **Register.**

   Compare the tone, or register, of the following:

   a)   These apparent failures often result from inadequate planning and management, especially the lack of integration of biophysical and socio-economic information into the effort. The lack of integration of information is, in fact, a limitation that has been emphasised by many authors working with agricultural and land use planning in recent years (see, for instance, Vaughan et al., 1995; and Chidley and Brook, 1997).

   b)   It was routine – an ordinary minor operation – except for a single extraordinary point. The patient was on an operating table in Milan. The doctors were in Washington, nearly 6,000 kilometres away. The news that, for the first time, a transatlantic operation had been carried out with a robot doctor in one continent copying the real-time hand movements of a live doctor in another, introduces a new medical age.

   c)   Legislation identifies the minimum space of 11 m^3 that should be allocated to each person and should be adhered to especially if much of the room is taken up with essential furniture. Equally, the maximum height of a room is now accepted for such calculations as three metres. For example, in a room 5 m $\times$ 4 m $\times$ 3 m (high) this would provide initial space for five persons.

The first extract is an example of **academic** register, used, for instance, in dissertations and academic journals. This typically uses cautious language like *apparent* and *often*, as well as academic vocabulary (*biophysical, socio-economic*), and will generally include references.

The second passage is **journalistic**. The first part attempts to interest the reader by presenting the story in a simple but dramatic way (*a single extraordinary point*). The importance of the news item is stressed by the claim *a new medical age*. Journalism often uses current idioms like *real time*.

The last extract uses a very **formal** tone, suitable for a semi-legal text. Verbs such as *identifies*, *adhered to* and *allocated*, the use of passives (*be allocated*), and special vocabulary (*persons* instead of the more normal *people*) are typical of this register.

cross reference

2.10   *Style*
3.6   *Formality in Verbs*

4. **Although it can be acceptable to use articles from newspapers, magazines and the internet, which are often more accessible and up to date, in academic work students need to be aware that these sources may have less credibility, and that material written for a wider readership tends to be less detailed.**

   Students need to be especially careful of taking journalistic phrases and using them in formal essays.

5. *Read the following texts and analyse the register in each case, by giving examples of the language used.*

a) Wherever possible complaints should be handled at a local level and without recourse to unduly formal proceedings. It is therefore essential that all staff who have contact with students are aware of the relevant procedures and are empowered to resolve issues as they arise. Staff dealing with complaints are encouraged, whenever practical, to meet with the complainant. Face-to-face discussions are often very helpful to establish the precise cause of dissatisfaction, to explore the remedy sought by the complainant and to foster a mutual understanding of the issues.

b) Studies of childhood imaginary companions have not yielded clear interactions with age and creativity. It could be suggested that the common assumption of imaginary companions being mainly a preschool phenomenon may have encouraged studies to use very young children as participants. In their review of the literature, Pearson and Mayer (1998) concluded that the experience of imaginary companions peaked in children aged between 2.5 and 3.5 years.

c) Amazing recent research by David Storey of Warwick University shows that businesses started by older people last longer than those started by younger entrepreneurs. He discovered that 70% of firms started by 50–55-year-olds survived for over three years, but only 30% for those of the 20–25 age group. As the numbers of old folk are increasing rapidly, such 'grey entrepreneurs' are likely to become more common. But what's the secret of their remarkable success rate?

Text	Register	Examples
a		
b		
c		

5.   Selecting Key Points

After selecting and understanding the most relevant texts, the next step is usually to make notes on the sections of the texts that relate to your topic. Units 5–8 practise this process, which involves a number of inter-linked skills.

cross reference

1.6 Note-Making

1. **The first stage of note-making is to identify the key points in the text for your purpose.**

   Study the following example (key points in italic).

   WHY WOMEN LIVE LONGER

   Despite the overall increase in life expectancy *in Britain* over the past century, *women still live significantly longer than men.* In fact, in 1900 men could expect to live to 49 and women to 52, a difference of three years, while *now the figures are 74 and 79*, which shows that the gap has increased to five years. *Various reasons have been suggested for this situation*, such as the possibility that men may die earlier because they take more risks. But a team of British *scientists have recently found a likely answer in the immune system*, which protects the body from diseases. *The thymus is the organ which produces the T cells* which actually combat illnesses. Although both sexes suffer from deterioration of the thymus as they age, *women appear to have more T cells in their bodies than men of the same age*. It is this, the scientists believe, that *gives women better protection* from potentially fatal diseases such as influenza and pneumonia.

   Having selected these sections of the text, you can then go on to make notes from them:

   > British women live longer than men: 79/74
   >
   > reasons? new research suggests immune system > thymus > T cells
   >
   > women have more T cells than men = better protection

2. *Read the following and then choose a suitable title that expresses the key point.*

   TITLE: ....

   Dean Kamen is a 50-year-old American eccentric who is also a multi-millionaire. He always wears blue denim shirts and jeans, even when visiting his friend, the president, in the White House. He flies to work by helicopter, which he also uses for visiting his private island off the coast of Connecticut. As an undergraduate Kamen developed the first pump that would give regular doses of medicine to patients. The patent for this and other original medical inventions has produced a huge income, allowing him to run his own research company which, among many other projects, has produced the iBot, the world's first wheelchair which can climb stairs.

3. *In the following text, three key points are in italic. Decide on their order of importance.*

   HOT RUBBISH

   a) *The majority of people in the small Derbyshire village of Poolsbrook have joined a scheme to make power from rubbish.* b)*Methane gas will be collected from the local rubbish tip and will be used to heat houses more cheaply and generate electricity.* The villagers, who have been affected by the closure of the local coal mines, suffer from unemployment, so cheap heating is especially important for them. They have raised the £2 million cost from development agencies. c)*The new system*, which will be the first of its kind in Europe, *will lead to a healthier environment by cutting CO_2 emissions*, and should also create three full-time jobs.

1) ....
2) ....
3) ....

4. *Underline four key points in the following text.*

THE SIXTH WAVE?

Lord May, the president of the Royal Society, has claimed that the world is facing a wave of extinctions similar to the five mass extinctions of past ages. He calculates that the current rate of extinction is between 100 and 1,000 times faster than the historical average. The cause of previous extinctions, such as the one which killed the dinosaurs, is uncertain, but was probably an external event such as collision with a comet.

However the present situation is caused by human consumption of plants, which has resulted in a steady increase in agriculture and a consequent reduction in habitat for animals. Although many people are still hungry, food production has increased by 100% since 1965.

Lord May also pointed out that it was very difficult to make accurate estimates as nobody knew how many species of animals lived on the planet. So far 1.5 million species had been named, but the true figure might be as high as 100 million. Our ignorance of this made it almost impossible to work out the actual rate of extinction. However, the use of intelligent guesses suggests that losses over the past century were comparable with the extinctions of earlier periods, evidence of which is found in the fossil record.

5. **When preparing to write an essay you may be concerned with only one aspect of a text, so your key points should relate only to the topic you are examining.**

    a) *You are preparing to write an essay on 'Marketing – art or science?' Read the text below and underline the sections relevant to your essay.*

BOTTLED WATER UNDER ATTACK

The Water Companies Association (WCA) has claimed that bottled water costs 700 times more than tap water, but is often of inferior quality. The chief executive of the WCA pointed out that although bottled water advertising often associated the product with sport and health there was no truth in this link. The reality, she said, was that the packaging of bottled water was environmentally damaging, since millions of empty bottles had to be disposed of in rubbish tips. 2% of samples of bottled water failed a purity test conducted by the Drinking Water Inspectorate, while only 0.3% of tap water samples failed the same test. Labels on bottled water often referred to 'spring' and 'natural water', which were meaningless phrases. In addition, bottled water was imported from as far as Korea and Kenya, which was a waste of resources. These criticisms, however, were rejected by the British Soft Drinks Association, which argued that bottled water was a successful business founded on giving the customers choice, quality and convenience.

b) *You are preparing an essay on 'The application of DNA research to the development of vaccines'. Read the text and underline the relevant sections.*

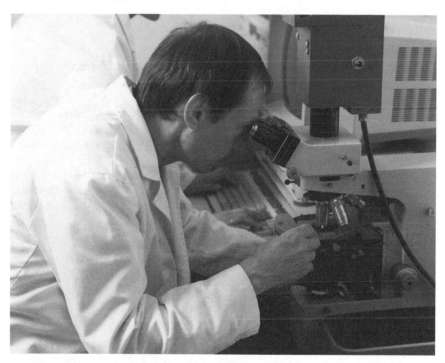

NEW LIGHT ON THE PLAGUE

The plague, which first struck Europe in the sixth century, was one of the great disasters of history. In the fourteenth century it became the Black Death, when it may have killed one third of the entire population. The microbe that causes the disease lives on rats, and is passed on to humans by the bite of a flea. It still survives today, though outbreaks are less deadly: the World Health Organisation receives reports of 3,000 cases annually. Scientists believe that the microbe was originally a stomach infection, but evolved into a more lethal disease about 1,500 years ago.

Now the genetic code of the plague bacterium has been 'read' by scientists; a total of 465 million 'letters' of DNA. They believe that this will help in the development of vaccines for the plague, one of which has begun clinical trials. In parts of Africa drug-resistant strains of the disease have evolved, which gives added importance to the work, as does the threat that the plague might be used as an agent of bacteriological warfare.

6.   Note-Making

Effective note-making is a key writing skill, with a number of practical uses. Good note-making techniques lead to accurate essays. Although you are the only person who will read your notes, clarity and organisation are still important.

1. **What are the main reasons for note-making?**
   Add to the ideas below.
   a) to avoid plagiarism
   b) ....
   c) ....
   d) ....

2. **Effective note-making is part of a sequence.**
   What comes before and after?

| | NOTE-MAKING | |

3. *You are writing an essay on 'Conservation at sea'. You find the following article in a magazine called* **Science South**, *volume 27 (2002). The author is J. Doyle. Read the text (key points in italic) and make notes.*

STUDYING SQUID

Before the British occupation of *the Falkland Islands* in 1833 most of the sailors who went there were mainly interested in collecting oil and skins from the whales, seals and penguins which flourished in the South Atlantic. The British introduced sheep farming, but since this became less profitable after the 1960s the islanders have been forced to pay more attention to the contents of the island waters.

These waters are rich in squid, and the sale of fishing licences for this harvest has funded research to allow the stocks to be managed efficiently. There are two kinds of squid around the Falklands; Illex is eaten in East Asia, while Loligo is popular in Spain. The latter was found to breed at two periods in the year; one season is May to July and the other is October and November. This second period, which is summer in the South Atlantic, coincides with the local penguin breeding season and makes the baby squid more vulnerable. As a result, the scientists suggested that the fishing season for Loligo should be postponed for a few months to allow the stock to recover, and when this was done the fishermen found that they had a better catch than before.

The other squid, Illex, was found to have a different pattern, swimming south from Brazil to the Falklands in summer, and then back north again. To deal with a species that migrates through the waters of several countries it has been necessary to set up an agreement between the governments concerned to restrict the fishing season in order to allow squid numbers to build up.

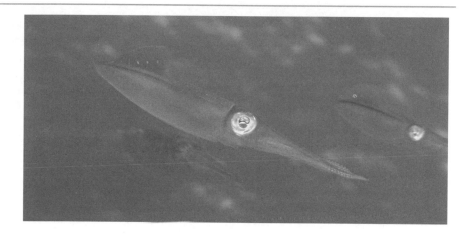

cross reference

2.9 *References and Quotations*
3.1 *Abbreviations*

4. A set of notes for your essay might look like this:

> Source: Doyle, J. (2002) *Science South* **27** pp. 24–28.
> Falkland Islands – research programme found:
>
> SQUID → a) *Illex* (E. Asia) – N/S migration pattern from Brazil
>   b) *Loligo* (Spain) – breeds   i)   May – July
>   ii) Oct – Nov
>
> suggested:
> a) postpone Loligo fishing (improved catch)
> b) restrict Illex fishing by int. agreement

Note the use of headings, listings, abbreviations ('N/S') and symbols. You need to develop your own style for note-making, as you will have to read them later. Do not abbreviate too much, or you may find the notes impossible to understand in the future.

5. *You have been told to write an essay on 'Malaria – can it be controlled?' You decide to make notes on the following article from a magazine called **Medical Report** (Volume 34 1998, pp. 78–86). The author's name is Irene Nemecova. Make notes on the whole text in the box below.*

MALARIA FIGHTS BACK

Drug-resistant strains of malaria, already one of the world's major killers, are steadily spreading across the globe. The deadly strains have established themselves in South East Asia and South America, and have recently begun to spread across India and Africa. Formerly under control in many areas, the disease now threatens two billion people living in more than 100 countries.

Estimates suggest that there are now more than 350 million cases of malaria a year – a total four times the level of the early 1970s. In Africa alone the disease kills one million children each year.

Several factors are responsible for this disturbing development. Spreading world poverty has deprived nations of funds for sanitation, so that many health projects have been stopped, while increased movements of migrant workers and tourists have carried infections more rapidly from one country to another. At the same time, the overuse of drugs, especially antibiotics, has led to the establishment of resistant strains of diseases.

As well as this, hopes that genetic engineers might soon develop the world's first malaria vaccine, a long-sought goal, have been questioned recently by several scientists. 'There are so many strains of malaria parasite,' said one scientist, 'and each is able to alter its chemical surface and trick its way past the body's defences. We'd need a remarkable vaccine to cope with that. However, a malaria vaccine is now undergoing human trials and may be available for use if proved successful.'

6. *You are preparing to write an essay on 'The impact of climate on history'. The text below is taken from page 221 of a book called* **Volcanic Disasters** *by E.B. Pitnam, published in 1993. Underline the relevant points and make notes.*

One of the greatest explosions in modern history occurred in 1815, when an Indonesian volcano called Mt. Tambora blew up. The eruption involved about 100 cubic kilometres of material being blown into the sky, with huge loss of life both on land and sea. Large quantities of volcanic dust were ejected into the atmosphere, and this dust gradually spread around the world, causing alarming events on the other side of the world.

In New England in north eastern USA farmers were hit by bitterly cold weather in June and July 1816. Much of the harvest was lost due to repeated waves of frost and snow in the middle of summer. The same pattern was recorded in Europe, where agriculture was still suffering the effects of the Napoleonic Wars. In France wheat prices reached their highest point of the century in 1817.

As European demand for food rose, prices doubled in America. Although some profited from the shortages, others were driven to emigrate into the unexplored lands to the west. Numbers leaving Vermont, for example, increased by 100% between 1816–17.

7.   Paraphrasing

Paraphrasing involves changing a text so that it is quite dissimilar to the source yet retains all the meaning. This skill is useful in several areas of academic work, but this unit focuses on using paraphrasing in note-making and summary writing. Effective paraphrasing is vital in academic writing to avoid the risk of plagiarism.

1. **Although paraphrasing techniques are used in summary writing, paraphrasing does not aim to shorten the length of a text, merely to restate the text.**

   For example,

   Evidence of a lost civilisation has been found off the coast of China.

   could be paraphrased:

   Remains of an ancient society have been discovered in the sea near China.

---

cross reference

2.11   Synonyms

---

2. **A good paraphrase is significantly different from the wording of the original, without altering the meaning at all.**

   Read the text below and then decide which is the best paraphrase, (a) or (b).

   Ancient Egypt collapsed in about 2180 BC. Studies conducted of the mud from the River Nile showed that at this time the mountainous regions which feed the Nile suffered from a prolonged drought. This would have had a devastating effect on the ability of Egyptian society to feed itself.

   a) The sudden ending of Egyptian civilisation over 4,000 years ago was probably caused by changes in the weather in the region to the south. Without the regular river flooding there would not have been enough food.

   b) Research into deposits of the Egyptian Nile indicate that a long dry period in the mountains at the river's source may have led to a lack of water for irrigation around 2180BC, which was when the collapse of Egyptian society began.

3. *Techniques.*

   a) Changing vocabulary:

   studies > research

   society > civilisation

   mud > deposits

   b) Changing word class:

   Egypt (n.) > Egyptian (adj.)

   mountainous regions (adj. + n.) > in the mountains (n.)

   c) Changing word order:

   Ancient Egypt collapsed > the collapse of Egyptian society began

4. *Find synonyms for the words in italic.*

   a) Sleep *scientists* have found that *traditional remedies* for insomnia, *such as* counting sheep, *are ineffective*.

   Example:

   Sleep *researchers* have found that *established cures* for insomnia, *for instance* counting sheep, *do not work*.

b)   Instead, they have *found* that *imagining a pleasant scene* is likely to *send you to* sleep *quickly*.

c)   The *research team divided* 50 insomnia sufferers into three groups.

d)   One group *was told to imagine* a waterfall, while another group *tried* sheep counting.

5. *Change the word class of the words in italic, and then re-write the sentences.*

a)   A third group was given no *special instructions* about going to sleep.

Example:

A third group was not specially instructed about going to sleep.

b)   It was *found* that the group thinking of waterfalls fell asleep 20 minutes quicker.

c)   Mechanical tasks like counting sheep are *apparently* too boring to make people sleepy.

6. *Change the word order of the following sentences.*

a)   There are many practical applications to research into insomnia.

Example:

Research into insomnia has many practical applications.

b)   About one in ten people are thought to suffer from severe insomnia.

c)   It is calculated that the cost of insomnia for the American economy may be $35 billion a year.

7. *Combine all these techniques to paraphrase the paragraph as fully as possible.*

Sleep scientists have found that traditional remedies for insomnia, such as counting sheep, are ineffective. Instead, they have found that imagining a pleasant scene is likely to send you to sleep quickly. The research team divided 50 insomnia sufferers into three groups. One group imagined watching a waterfall, while another group tried sheep counting. A third group was given no special instructions about going to sleep. It was found that the group thinking of waterfalls fell asleep 20 minutes quicker. Mechanical tasks like counting sheep are apparently too boring to make people sleepy. There are many practical applications for research into insomnia. About one in ten people are thought to suffer from severe insomnia. It is calculated that the cost of insomnia for the American economy may be $35 billion a year.

8. *Use the same techniques to paraphrase the following text.*

Before the last century no humans had visited Antarctica, and even today the vast continent has a winter population of less than 200 people. However, a recent report from a New Zealand government agency outlines the scale of the pollution problem in the ice and snow. Although untouched compared with other regions in the world, the bitter cold of Antarctica means that the normal process of decay is prevented. As a result some research stations are surrounded by the rubbish of nearly 60 years' operations.

Despite popular belief, the polar continent is really a desert, with less precipitation than the Sahara. In the past, snowfall slowly covered the waste left behind, like beer cans or dead ponies, but now, possibly due to global warming, the ice is thinning and these are being exposed. Over 10 years ago the countries using Antarctica agreed a treaty on waste disposal, under which everything is to be taken home, and this is slowly improving the situation. However, the scientists do not want everything removed. The remains of very early expeditions at the beginning of the twentieth century have acquired historical value and will be preserved.

8.   Summary Writing

Making summaries is a common activity in everyday life. If a friend asks us about a book we are reading, we do not tell them about everything in the book. Instead, we make a summary of the most interesting and important aspects. The same principle applies to summarising in academic writing.

1. *Choose four of the topics below and write summaries in no more than twelve words each.*

   Example:

   Birmingham is a large industrial city in the English West Midlands.

   a)   Your home town

   b)   Bill Gates

   c)   Your academic subject

   d)   The last book you read

   e)   A film you saw recently

   f)   Your mother/father

   Look at the summaries you have written above. What are the features of a successful summary?

2. **Summary writing is an important skill in academic work.**

   Different kinds of summaries are needed in different situations.

   List as many study uses for summary writing as you can think of.

   making notes from lectures

   ....

   ....

3. **In essay writing students often have to summarise part of a book or journal article.**

   The summary may be just one or two sentences, to explain the main idea of the article, and perhaps compare it with another summarised text, or it might be necessary to include much more detail. In other words, a summary can range from 1–2% of the original to more than 50%: summarising is a flexible tool.

   At first students need to follow a series of steps to summarise successfully. With practice the number of steps may be reduced, as the process becomes more automatic.

   Complete the list of stages in a successful summary.

   a)   Read the text carefully and check key vocabulary.

   b)   Underline or highlight the ....

   c)   Make notes of these, taking care to ....

   d)   Write the summary using the notes, re-organising the ....

   e)   Check the summary to make sure no .... have been omitted or distorted.

4. *Read the following text and compare the summaries. Decide which is best, giving reasons.*

Researchers in France and the United States have recently reported that baboons are able to think abstractly. It has been known for some time that chimpanzees are capable of abstract thought, but baboons are a more distant relation to mankind. In the experiment, scientists trained two baboons to use a personal computer and a joystick. The animals had to match computer designs which were basically the same but had superficial differences. The baboons performed better than would be expected by chance. The researchers describe their study in an article in the *Journal of Experimental Psychology*.

a) French and American scientists have shown that baboons have the ability to think in an abstract way. The animals were taught to use a computer, and then had to select similar patterns, which they did at a rate better than chance.

b) Baboons are a kind of monkey more distant from man than chimpanzees. Although it is known that chimpanzees are able to think abstractly, until recently it was not clear if baboons could do the same. But new research has shown that this is so.

c) According to a recent article in the *Journal of Experimental Psychology*, baboons are able to think in an abstract way. The article describes how researchers trained two baboons to use a personal computer and a joystick. The animals did better than would be expected.

cross reference

1.5 Selecting Key Points

5. *Read the following text and underline the key points.*

Indian researchers are trying to find out if there is any truth in old sayings which claim to predict the weather. In Gujarat farmers have the choice of planting either peanuts, which are more profitable in wet years, or castor, which does better in drier conditions. The difference depends on the timing of the monsoon rains, which can arrive at any time between the beginning and the middle of June. Farmers, however, have to decide what seeds to sow in April or May.

There is a local saying, at least a thousand years old, which claims that the monsoon starts 45 days after the flowering of a common tree, *Cassia fistula*. Dr Kanani, an agronomist from Gujarat Agricultural University, has been studying the relationship since 1996, and has found that the tree does successfully predict the approximate date of the monsoon's arrival.

6. *Complete the following notes of the key points.*
   a) Indian scientists checking ancient...
   b) Old saying links monsoon to ....
   c) Used by farmers to select peanuts (for wet) or ....
   d) Dr Kanani of Gujarat Agricultural University has found that ....
       ....

cross reference

3.5 *Conjunctions*

7. *Link the notes together to make a complete summary using conjunctions where necessary. Check the final text for factual accuracy.*

Indian scientists are checking ....

8. *The original text was about 150 words. The summary above is about 50, so the original has been reduced by about 65%. However, it might be necessary to summarise still further. Using the same techniques, summarise the summary in about 20 words.*

9. Combining Sources

Most essays require the writer to read more than one book or article. The differences between the ideas of different writers may be the focus of the essay. This unit examines ways of presenting such contrasting views.

cross reference

2.9   *References and Quotations*
3.16   *Referring Verbs*

1. *Read the example, from a study of women's experience of prison.*

   According to Giallombardo (1966), women alleviated the pains of imprisonment by developing kinship links with other inmates. Similarly Heffernan (1972) *found* that adaptation to prison was facilitated by the creation of a pseudo-family. Owen (1998) also *notes* that the female sub-culture is based on personal relationships with other women inmates. Others, however, *believe* that the subculture in women's prisons is undergoing a gradual shift that more closely resembles that of male prisons. Fox (1982) *states*, for example, that the cooperative caring prison community that has embodied characterizations of female prisons has evolved into a more dangerous and competitive climate.

   a) How many writers are mentioned?
   b) What is the function of the words in italics?
   c) What phrase is used to mark the point in the text where there is a shift from one point of view to another?

2. *Below are two sources used for an essay titled 'Should genetically modified (GM) foods have a role in future agriculture?' Read the sources first, then the essay extract.*

SOURCE A

Genetic modification (GM) is the most recent application of biotechnology to food, which can also be called genetic engineering or genetic manipulation. The phrase 'Genetically Modified Organisms' or GMOs is used frequently in the scientific literature to describe plants and animals which have had DNA introduced into them by means other than the 'natural' process of an egg and a sperm.

New species have always evolved through natural selection by means of random genetic variation. Early farmers used this natural variation to selectively breed wild animals, plants and even micro-organisms such as yogurt cultures and yeasts. They produced domesticated variants better suited to the needs of humans, long before the scientific basis for the process was understood. Despite this long history of careful improvement, such procedures are now labelled 'interfering with nature'.

SOURCE B

Genetic modification (GM) is in fact far more than a mere development of selective breeding techniques. Combining genetic material from species that cannot breed naturally is an interference in areas which may be highly dangerous. The consequences of this kind of manipulation cannot be foreseen.

It seems undeniable that these processes may lead to major benefits in food production and the environment. There is no doubt, for example, that some medical advances may have saved millions of lives. However, this level of technology can contain a strong element of risk.

Our ignorance of the long-term effects of releasing GM plants or even animals into the environment means that this step should only be taken after very careful consideration.

ESSAY EXTRACT

It has been claimed that GM technology is no different from breeding techniques which have been practised by man for thousands of years. Source A states that this process is similar to natural selection and remarks: 'such procedures are now labelled "interfering with nature"'. On the other hand Source B considers that, although GM technology could bring considerable benefits in medicine and agriculture, it is quite different to traditional processes of selection. He believes that crossing the species barrier is a dangerous step and that there is insufficient knowledge of the long-term results of such developments.

3. **The essay writer uses a mixture of direct quotes and summaries of arguments.**
   a) *Find an example of each.*
   b) *What phrase does the writer use to mark the point where he moves from dealing with Source A to Source B?*
   c) *List all the phrases used to introduce summaries.*

   It has been claimed that ....

4. *You are preparing to write an essay titled 'The social effects of tourism in developing countries'. Read the sources and then complete the paragraph comparing their views.*

SOURCE C

When countries begin to provide facilities for mass tourism, such as hotels and leisure complexes, there is an immediate demand for labour. Work is created for cleaners, waiters, gardeners and drivers on a scale which may significantly boost the local economy. Such work may provide opportunities to learn valuable new skills. For many, these semi-skilled jobs provide an attractive alternative to subsistence agriculture or fishing, while at the same time the tax revenues from their earnings increase the national income.

SOURCE D

One inevitable feature of tourism's growth is the creation of badly-paid, seasonal jobs in holiday resorts. Much of this work combines insecurity with long hours of work in poor conditions. In Thailand, for example, there are cases of hotel maids working 15 hour days for less than $4. Moreover, the combination of wealthy tourists being served by exploited waitresses is likely to increase social tensions in these areas. Another risk is that natural or human disasters such as wars and earthquakes may drive visitors away without warning, leaving tens of thousands unemployed.

SOURCE E

It has been claimed that the development of tourism played a major part in helping to modernise parts of Franco's Spain in the 1960s. The presence of easy-going, affluent visitors apparently encouraged the locals to learn new skills and open new businesses. Despite this positive interpretation, many examples could be presented where the arrival of rich and idle tourists has been an encouragement for crime, prostitution and other less desirable aspects of the modern economy. Much seems to depend on the economic alternatives offered by the society, and of course the scale of tourist arrivals.

It has been argued that tourism can have a very positive social influence on a developing country.

10. Planning a Text

Outline planning was examined in Unit 2. Planning gives essays a coherent structure and, most importantly, helps to ensure that they answer the question set. Although all essays need planning, they are written in two different situations: as coursework, and in exams. Clearly, under the time pressure of an exam, planning is more hurried, but also more critical. This unit looks at planning first in exams and then for coursework.

cross reference

1.2   *Developing Plans from Titles*

1. **In the case of essays written in exams, it is best to begin planning by analysing the title and then writing down any ideas that seem relevant.**

   This process is called **brainstorming**, and at first ideas are collected in any order.

   Read the title below and add more ideas to the list.

   Tourism is the world's most important industry. Why is this, and will it continue to be so?

   > development of jet aircraft
   >
   > mass tourism began in the 1960s
   >
   > increased leisure time in rich countries
   >
   > problems of overcrowding, pollution
   >
   > . . . .
   >
   > . . . .
   >
   > . . . .
   >
   > . . . .

cross reference

1.12   *Organising the Main Body*
2.5   *Discussion*

2. **Having assembled your ideas, it is then necessary to find a suitable framework for the essay.**

   A structure may be suggested by the title of the essay. There are a number of common structures used in essay writing.

   Which would be most suitable for the title above?

   a) **Time** – usually from the past to the present or the future, as in a story.

   b) **Comparison** – two or more topics are examined and compared, one after another.

   c) **For and against** – the advantages and disadvantages of two systems are discussed.

3. *Complete the plan for the title in (1) using ideas from (1).*

   a) Introduction: historical background/current problems, e.g. overcrowding

   b) Main body:

   i)   mass tourism began in 1960s with development of jet aircraft

   ii)

   iii)

   iv)

   c) Conclusion:

4. *Decide which of the three frameworks in (2) would be most suitable for the following titles.*
   a)   Prisons make criminals worse, and should be abolished – Discuss.
   b)   In the UK, radio is gaining audience while TV is losing viewers. Consider possible reasons.
   c)   Trace the development of mass production and evaluate its main benefits.
   d)   'Examinations can never be fair.' To what extent is this true?
   e)   The internet will make books redundant in twenty years – Discuss.

cross reference

2.3   *Comparisons*

5. *Study the title below and the ideas collected for the essay. Add to the list if possible. Then choose a suitable framework and complete the plan below.*
   Compare the effects of advertising on TV with advertising in newspapers. What are the main differences? Are there any similarities?

   TV adverts more lively, dynamic

   newspaper adverts can be targeted at a special market, e.g. local

   TV advertising very expensive (to make and show)

   many people video TV and fast-forward adverts

   newspaper adverts can be prepared more quickly

   TV adverts can reach a wider audience

   ....

   a)   Introduction: role of newspapers and TV in society today
   b)   Main body:
        i)
        ii)
        iii)
        iv)
   c)   Conclusion:

6. *Choose one of the titles below and note at least six ideas that might be used in the essay. Then select a suitable framework and write a plan.*
   a)   In twenty years' time most learning will be online. The internet will replace the classroom.
   b)   Describe the education system in your country and suggest how it could be improved.

7. **In the case of longer essays, written as coursework, planning will normally be a two-stage process:**

a) before reading: using the title to develop an outline structure

b) after reading: modifying the outline and adding detail

Study the plan below. Suggest how it could be modified/improved.

Title: Analyse the role of the private sector in the modern English education system.

a) 550,000 children at private schools in England & Wales

b) Negative effects on state system – better pupils removed

c) 7% of all pupils in England & Wales attend private schools

d) Reasons for using private sector, e.g. smaller classes, better results in exams

e) 20% of university intake from private schools

f) Positive effects on state system – fewer pupils to teach/provides competition

11. Organising Paragraphs

Paragraphs are the basic building blocks of texts. Well-organised paragraphs not only help readers understand the argument; they also help writers to structure their ideas effectively.

1. *Read the following paragraph.*

The way we use banks is currently changing. This is partly because of the introduction of new technology in the last ten years. The personal computer and the internet, for instance, allow customers to view their accounts at home and perform operations such as moving money between accounts. At the same time banks are being reorganised in ways that affect both customers and staff. In the past five years over 3,000 bank branches have closed in Britain. The banks have discovered that staffing call centres is cheaper than running a branch network.

The structure of the paragraph is:

1. topic sentence	The way we use banks …
2. reason	This is partly because …
3. example	The personal computer …
4. details	At the same time banks …
5. further details	In the past five …
6. reason	The banks have discovered …

cross reference

2.4   *Definitions*
2.6   *Examples*

2. **A paragraph is a collection of sentences that deal with one subject.**

   All paragraphs contain a **topic** sentence, which is often, but not always, the first. Other components vary according to the nature of the topic. Introductory paragraphs often contain **definitions**, and descriptive paragraphs include a lot of **detail**. Other sentences give **examples** and offer **reasons** and **restatements**.

3. *Read and analyse the following paragraph.*

   In recent years all British universities have adopted the semester system. A semester is a period of time which lasts for half the academic year. Semester 1, for example, starts in September and finishes in January. Previously the academic year had been divided into three terms: autumn, winter and spring. Most courses consist of modules that last for one semester, and exams are held at the end of each. Britain began using semesters to make it easier for international students to move from one country to another.

1.	
2.	
3.	
4.	
5.	
6.	

4. *The sentences below make up a paragraph, but have been mixed up. Use the table to re-write the sentences in the correct order.*

a) For many centuries it has been the centre of the country's economic, cultural and social life.

b) 500 years ago it had become a major river port for ships trading with Europe.

c) Its dominance is due to its strategic site near the lowest crossing point of the River Thames.

d) London has been the English capital for over 1000 years.

1. topic	
2. restatement	
3. reason	
4. detail	

cross reference

2.2   *Cohesion*

5. *The sentences below form a paragraph, but they have been mixed up. Rewrite them in the box overleaf in the correct order and analyse the paragraph structure.*

a) This was because of problems with the roof design.

b) Mark Roberts will watch a display of jazz dance and disco.

c) The opening has been delayed by almost three months.

d) The new Leisure Centre will be opened on May 15th by the Sports Minister.

e) The architects are currently being sued for £2 m. by the local council.

1.	
2.	
3.	
4.	
5.	

cross reference

1.13   Introductions

6. *You are writing an essay on 'Prisons make criminals worse, and should be abolished'. Using the notes below, complete the introductory paragraph, following the structure provided.*

Introduction

Modern prison system developed in 19th century

Prisons intended to isolate, punish and reform

Steep rise in number of prisoners in last 20 years

Critics claim they are 'university of crime'

Essay aims to consider how effective prisons are

1. **detail**	The modern prison system
2. **reason**	The system had three basic aims:
3. **detail**	In the last 20 years
4. **detail**	Prisons are commonly criticised
5. **topic**	This essay attempts to evaluate

cross reference

2.5   *Discussion*

7. *Using the second set of notes, write the next paragraph of the essay.*

Advantages

prisons offer society three apparent benefits

provide punishment by deprivation of freedom

offenders are segregated so cannot re-offend

possibility of reform through training programmes

1. topic	
2. detail	
3. detail	
4. detail	

8. *Using the next set of notes, write the third paragraph.*

Drawbacks

Prisons appear to be failing in 21st century

Prison population steadily rising in many countries

Many prisoners are 'repeat offenders'

Few prisons able to offer effective reform programmes

Prison conditions often brutal and degrading

1. topic	
2.	
3.	
4.	
5.	

12. Organising the Main Body

This and the next two units deal with the organisation of the main body, the introduction and the conclusion. In the case of longer assignments it is often better to write the main body before the introduction. With shorter essays, for example in exams, this is impractical, and the introduction has to be written first.

1. **The structure of the main body depends on the length of the essay and the subject of study.**

   Longer essays may include the following sections:

   Experimental set-up – a technical description of the organisation of an experiment

   Methods – how the research was carried out

   Findings/results – what was discovered by the research/experiment

   Case study – a description of an example of the topic being researched

   Discussion – an examination of the issues and the writer's verdict

2. *The sections below comprise the main body of an essay titled 'Studying abroad: an analysis of costs and benefits'. Decide on the heading of each section and the best order for them.*

   a) Comparisons of the advantages and disadvantages that students mentioned about study abroad and an attempt to decide if most students benefited from the experience.

   b) Detailed description of the survey carried out by the researcher.

   c) An extensive study of two students (from different cultures) studying in Britain who were interviewed by the researcher.

   d) A report of what the survey found, with statistical analysis.

1.10 *Planning a Text*

3. **Shorter essays (in exams, for example) tend to have simpler structures:**

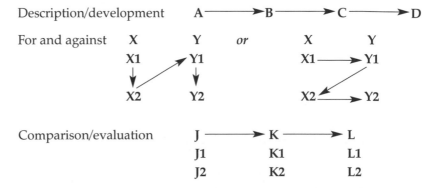

Description/development   A ——→ B ——→ C ——→ D

For and against   X   Y   *or*   X   Y
                  X1   ↗ Y1   X1 ——→ Y1
                  ↓ ↗ ↓   ↗
                  X2   Y2   X2 ——→ Y2

Comparison/evaluation   J ——→ K ——→ L
                          J1   K1   L1
                          J2   K2   L2

Match the examples of plans for main bodies below to the structures above.

a) Prisons make criminals worse, and should be abolished – Discuss.

   i) benefit of prisons – deterrence

   ii) benefit of prisons – removes dangerous people from society

      iii) drawback of prisons – prisoners lose contact with non-criminal society

      iv) drawback of prisons – prisoners become bitter and learn criminal techniques

  b) In the UK, radio is gaining audience while TV is losing viewers. Consider possible reasons.

      i) radio can be listened to in many situations

      ii) radio offers a wide variety of programme types

      iii) radio does not demand full attention, e.g. background music

      iv) TV lacks flexibility, needs full attention

      v) economic factors: TV more expensive to buy/programmes more expensive to make

      vi) high production costs may result in poor quality of programmes

4. Inside the main body, ideas need to be presented in the most logical fashion, linked together to form a coherent argument.

Re-organise the notes below to achieve the best structure.

  a) Trace the development of the factory system and evaluate its social impact.

      workers forced to adopt a regular timetable to maintain production

      first factories employed unskilled workers; often women and children

      early employers enforced strict codes of discipline

      factories originally sited to make use of water power (in 18th C.)

      later some employers offered social benefits, e.g. housing/education

      in nineteenth century factories built near canals/railways for access to markets

  b) Lowering the minimum school leaving age to 14 would allow teachers to focus on teaching the students who wanted to be in school – Discuss.

      if they left at 14, students would be unlikely to find proper jobs

      some students more suited to work that doesn't require qualifications

      problem students waste everybody's time, including their own

      effort should be made in primary schools to prevent pupils falling behind

      many older students have lost interest in learning and disrupt classes

      in future, almost all jobs will demand academic skills

---

cross reference
3.5   Conjunctions

5. It is useful to mark the beginning of new paragraphs or the introduction of new subjects with special phrases.

To introduce a new paragraph/topic:

The main/chief factor/issue is ...

Turning to the subject of ...

Moving on to the question of ...

Another important area is ...

.... must also be examined

To add information inside a paragraph:

  a) Firstly, ...   The first point ...   In the first place ...

  b) Secondly, ...   Next, ...   Then, ...   In addition ...
      Moreover ...

  c) Finally, ...   Lastly,...

6. *Complete with suitable phrases the following extract from an essay on 'British weather'.*

The British are famous all over the world for their obsession with the weather, but in fact the reality is more complex than people often believe. This essay sets out to examine some of the principal influences on the weather of the British Isles.

.... is the geographical position of Britain, situated on the extreme western edge of the European continent. This means that a variety of weather types can dominate the country. .... the Atlantic Ocean can produce warm wet winds, especially in winter. .... the land mass of Europe can create anticyclonic weather, hot in summer and cold in winter. .... the polar region to the north can generate cold winds at most seasons of the year.

.... variations within Britain, there are significant differences between regions. .... the south of England can be much warmer than the north of Scotland, especially in winter. .... the west of Britain is usually much wetter than the east. .... even in the same district, hilly areas will be cooler and wetter than the lowlands.

.... is seasonal change, which in Britain is less distinct than in many countries. .... the Atlantic moderates extreme types of weather, and .... the weather pattern can change radically from year to year. As a result warm days in winter and chilly summer winds frequently surprise visitors to this country.

13. Introductions

An introduction is crucial, not just for what it says about the topic, but for what it tells the reader about the writer's style and approach. Unless you can introduce the subject clearly the reader may not wish to continue.

1. *What is the purpose of the introduction to an essay?*
   Choose from the items below:
   a) to define some of the terms in the title
   b) to give your opinion of the subject
   c) to show that you have read some research on the subject
   d) to show that the subject is worth writing about
   e) to explain which areas of the subject you will deal with
   f) to get the reader's attention with a provocative idea
   g) to show how you intend to organise your essay

cross reference
2.4 *Definitions*

2. **It may be necessary to clarify some of the words in the title.**

   This is to make it clear that you understand the title.

   Discuss the impact of privatisation on the British economy.

   Privatisation is the process of transferring certain industries from state control to the private sector, which began in Britain in 1981 with British Telecom …

3. **In longer assignments it is important to show that you are familiar with current research.**

   This can be demonstrated using phrases such as:

   A number of researchers have examined this issue, notably …

   Various investigations have explored the subject, especially …

4. **You must show the importance of the topic.**

   This can be either in the academic world or as a contemporary issue of wider relevance.

   As privatisation is increasingly seen as a remedy for economic ills in many other countries, it is worth examining its impact in Britain, which was a pioneer in this process.

5. **As you are writing only an essay, not a book, it is obviously not possible to deal with all aspects of your subject.**

   Therefore you need to explain what limits you are setting on the discussion, and possibly give reasons for this.

   Only privatisations completed between 1981 and 1992 will be dealt with, as it is too soon to assess the impact of later developments.

6. **For your own benefit, as well as the reader's, it is useful to outline how the essay will be organised.**

   An assessment will first be made of the performance of the privatised industries themselves, on an individual basis, and then the performance of the economy as a whole will be examined.

7. *Study the following extracts from introductions below and decide which of the functions in the box they fulfil.*

> i)   explain starting point for research
> ii) state aims/goals
> iii) refer to recent research in same area
> iv) give results of research
> v)   provide background information
> vi) concede limitations

a)   In many companies, the knowledge of most employees remains untapped for solving problems and generating new ideas.

b)   This paper positions Call Centres at the core of the mix of technologies public administration can use to innovate e-commerce.

c)   In fact, this is one of our main findings based on an extended sample period up to 1998.

d)   Admittedly, the tenor of my argument is tentative and exploratory.

e)   The purpose of this paper is to investigate changes in the incidence of extreme warm and cold temperatures over the globe since 1870.

f)   To what extent do increases in the food available per person at a national level contribute to reductions in child malnutrition? This question has generated a wide range of responses (Haddad et al., 1997).

8. **There is no such thing as a standard introduction, and much depends on the nature of the research and the length of the essay.**

However, for a relatively short essay written under exam conditions the following are worth including, in this order.

a)   Definitions of any terms in the title that are unclear

b)   Some background information

c)   Reference to other writers who have discussed this topic

d)   Your purpose in writing and the importance of the subject

e)   The points you are going to make/areas you are going to cover

cross reference

2.5   *Discussion*

9. *Prepare to write an introduction to an essay with the title 'Higher education should be available to everyone – Discuss' by answering the questions below.*

a)   Which terms in the title might need defining?

b)   What background information could you give?

c)   How can you show the relevance of this topic, in either Britain or another country?

d)   How are you going to limit your discussion, geographically, historically or both?

e)   How will you organise the main body of the essay?

As this is a short essay, it is not necessary to mention sources in the introduction.

10. *Write the introduction (about 100 words), using your answers from (9) and the notes provided below.*

definition	higher education (HE) = university education
background	increasing demand for HE worldwide puts pressure on national budgets > many states seek to shift costs to students
relevance	in most countries degree = key to better jobs & opportunities
discussion points	if sts. have to pay more of cost, discriminates against poorer families; how to keep HE open to able students from all backgrounds?

11. *Write an introduction to an essay on one of the following subjects, or choose a subject from your own discipline.*
    a) Compare the urbanisation process in the First and the Third Worlds.
    b) Assess the importance of public transport in the modern city.
    c) 'Lawyers are inflating the cost of medicine' – Discuss.
    d) To what extent is a democratic system necessary for economic development?

14. Conclusions

There is usually a link between the starting point, i.e. the title, and the conclusion. If the title is asking a question, the conclusion should contain the answer. The reader may look at the conclusion first to get a quick idea of the main arguments or points.

1. **Not every academic essay has a conclusion.**

   In some cases it may be linked to the discussion section, or it may be called *concluding remarks*, or *summary*. However, in most cases it is helpful for the reader to have a section that (quite briefly) looks back at what has been said and makes some comments about the main part.

   Read the following extracts from conclusions and match them with the list of functions in the box.

   a) In this review, attempts have been made to summarise and assess the current research trends of transgenic rice dealing exclusively with agronomically important genes.

   b) As always, this investigation has a number of limitations to be considered in evaluating its findings.

   c) Obviously, business expatriates could benefit from being informed that problem-focused coping strategies are more effective than symptom-focused ones.

   d) Another line of research worth pursuing further is to study the importance of language for expatriate assignments.

   e) Our review of 13 studies of strikes in public transport demonstrates that the effect of a strike on public transport ridership varies and may either be temporary or permanent.

   f) These results of the Colombia study reported here are consistent with other similar studies conducted in other countries (Baron & Norman, 1992).

   g) To be more precise, there was a positive relation between tolerant and patient problem solving and all four measures of adjustment: general, interaction, work and subjective well-being.

   h) To empirically test this conjecture, we need more cross-national replication of this research.

i)   comparisons with other studies
ii)   summary of main body
iii)   limitations of research
iv)   suggestions for further research
v)   practical implications and proposals

2. *Compare the following conclusions to two essays on 'Public transport in a modern economy'. Complete the table to show the main differences between them.*

a) As has been shown, public transport is likely to play an important role in the future. Despite possible changes in patterns of work and leisure, it seems possible that mass transport systems will remain necessary for the efficient movement of people. What is not clear is how such transport systems should be funded. Various schemes have been discussed, but the most effective model will probably contain some element of public funding. Market forces alone are unlikely to provide a satisfactory solution.

b) In such a brief study it is hard to draw definite conclusions about the future shape of public transport. The main areas of debate have been outlined, but much more research is needed before firm recommendations can be made. It can be seen that this is a controversial area, with strong protagonists on either side. Whether public transport flourishes or deteriorates in future is still unclear, though further studies may eventually suggest an answer.

a	
b	

3. *The following may be found in conclusions. Decide on the most suitable order for them (A–E).*

Implications of the findings

Proposals for further research

Limitations of the research

Reference to how these findings compare with other studies

Summary of main findings

4. *Below are notes for the main body of an essay. Read the notes and complete the conclusion, using your own ideas if necessary.*

Cultural adaptation among overseas students at a British university.

a) **The research programme**

purpose: to study how students from different cultural backgrounds adapt to academic life in the UK *size and method:* 250 questionnaires returned (30% Chinese, 25% SE Asian, 20% Middle Eastern, 25% other)

b) **Findings** – culture was only one factor in determining successful adaptation.

Other important factors: age/previous experience of living abroad/language proficiency

c) **Discussion** – how accurate was research? How could it have been improved? What can be done to help students adapt better?

summary	The aim of the study was to explore differing degrees of adjustment to life at a British university among overseas students from a variety of cultural backgrounds. 250 valid questionnaires were completed, representing about a third of the overseas student population, with significant numbers of Chinese, SE Asian and Middle Eastern students. The results suggest …………
implications	
limitations	
proposals for further research	

cross reference

4.4 Comparison Essay

5. *Study the notes for the essay below and write a conclusion in about 100 words.*

A comparison of classroom learning with internet-based teaching.

a) Reasons for increasing use of online education:

cheaper if large numbers involved

allows students to study in their own time

students do not have to travel to university

b) Reasons why classroom-based education remains popular:

students can be part of group; receive support and advice; learn from colleagues

students have face-to-face contact with a teacher

is seen as traditional and effective

c) Discussion

can a solitary student in front of a computer enjoy the same learning experience as a member of a class?

pressure of numbers in universities makes more online education likely

is internet learning really a new method of education? Distance learning has been popular for many years (e.g. Open University)

15. Re-reading and Re-writing

When you have finished the conclusion it may be tempting to hand in your work immediately. However, it is almost certain that it can be improved by being revised. With longer assignments, it may be worth asking a classmate to give an opinion.

1. **After finishing the first draft of an essay you should, if you have time, wait for a while and then re-read the essay, asking the following questions.**

   a) How well does this answer the question in the title?

   b) Have I forgotten any points that would strengthen the development?

   c) Is it clearly structured and well linked together?

cross reference

2.3   *Comparisons*

2. *Read this short essay written by a Japanese student to the title 'Compare the university system in your country with the British system'. Answer the questions above by making notes below.*

   It is said that there are large differences in the teaching methods between British universities and Japanese ones. Courses in British universities consist mainly of lectures, discussions, presentations and tutorials and students study specifically their major subject. On the other hand, Japanese universities normally have only lectures in the first two years and students have to study a wide range of subjects in addition to their major. The aim of this essay is to compare and analyse each system.

   In British universities, students need a more active attitude in their study than Japanese students. They need to prepare for presentations and discussions. This is useful for learning because they take much time for study outside the classroom and as they become familiar with their subjects they will become more interested in them.

   In Japan, students' attitude is amazingly passive and they study only just before exams.

   The other difference between British universities and Japanese ones is, as mentioned above, British students concentrate on their major subject and gain specific knowledge about it. Japanese students, however, gain wider knowledge by studying a few other subjects in addition to their major. This system gives students apparently much knowledge but they cannot study their major deeply and their knowledge is wide-ranging but not useful.

   In conclusion, British teaching methods give students more chance to know the subject thoroughly compared to Japanese teaching methods, but Japanese methods are suitable for students who are eager to gain a wide range of knowledge and like to study on their own. It is hard to say which is better, it depends on students.

   a) ....

   b) ....

   c) ....

3. **A careful re-reading of the essay would suggest the following points.**

   a) The essay only partly answers the title. It looks at university life from a student's position, but does not really deal with the system as a whole. The last line of the conclusion discusses a question not asked in the title.

   b) To deal with the subject more fully the writer needs to examine topics such as length of courses, funding of students, and admission procedures. If there is not space to discuss these in detail they must be at least mentioned, to show that the writer is aware that they are central to the subject.

   c) The introduction needs to be more general. It goes straight to a comparison of teaching methods. This could be in the main body. Otherwise the essay is well organised and quite logical.

cross reference

1.13   Introductions

4. *Use the notes below to re-write the introductory paragraph.*

   university education important in both UK & Japan (over 30% 18-year-olds)

   main points for comparison:

   a) admissions

   b) length of courses: 1st and higher degrees

   c) teaching methods

   d) assessment

   e) financial support

   essay will examine each point and analyse differences between countries

In both Britain and Japan, university education is undertaken by a significant number (about 30%) of all young people after leaving school.
....

cross reference

4.5   *Discursive Essay*

5. *Read this extract from the main body of an essay on 'Education is the most important factor in national development   Discuss'. Study the notes below and then re-write the extract.*

The need for education is crucial in any field. a) *It is something that no one can deny.* b) *The development in technology has provided us with many devices and machines that facilitate our lives. Nowadays, factories produce more in less time and that helps the economies of countries. The different scientific discoveries have improved the quality of life as well. The development in the medical field is an example; vaccines and antibiotics have saved many lives.* Take Japan, a country with few natural riches, where most of the land is mountains, but it is now one of the strongest countries economically. c) *The natural poverty of Japan has, in fact, been overcome by education* and it has become one of the most important countries in a short period of time.

a) This sentence repeats the idea in the first, but doesn't add anything new.

b) Not clear how this section relates to the subject. No clear link is established between education and technology.

c) The case for linking Japanese development and education is not established – the claim is too strong. Other factors need to be considered.

16. Proof-Reading

The vital final part of the writing process, proof-reading can prevent confusion and misunderstanding of your work. Although most word-processing programmes check your spelling, they will not detect other common types of mistakes.

cross reference

2.10 *Style*
3.9 *Nouns and Adjectives*
3.15 *Punctuation*
3.18 *Singular/Plural*
3.19 *Tenses*

1. **Before handing in any piece of written work for marking, it is important to check it carefully for errors that may distort your meaning or even make your work difficult to understand.**

   The following examples each contain **one** *common type of error. Underline the error and match it to the list of error types in the box.*

   > i) factual; ii) word ending; iii) punctuation; iv) tense;
   > v) vocabulary; vi) spelling; vii) singular/plural; viii) style;
   > ix) missing word; x) unnecessary word

   a) The natural poorness of Japan has been overcome …

   b) In 1980 in the United States there are 140,000 people who …

   c) Actually, hardly any of these has succeeded …

   d) … to choose the most suitable area in which they can success.

   e) Chinese history reflects in real social and cultural changes.

   f) The highest rate of imprisonment was regestred in the USA …

   g) Malaria is on the increase in countries such as Africa …

   h) I am very interested in German economy …

   i) … the french system is quite different.

   j) You don't always know which method is best.

2. **When proof-reading, it is a good idea to exchange texts with another student, since you may become over-familiar with your own work.**

   However, even in exam conditions, when this is not possible, it is vital to spend a few minutes checking through your work, for this may reveal careless errors that can be quickly corrected.

   Underline and correct the errors in the extracts below (one or two in each).

   a) The graph shows changes in the number of prisoners over five years (1930–1980).

   b) … the way the government prepares his citizens to contribute in the development ...

   c) Secondly, education not only teach people many knowledge …

   d) However, weather it is the most important factor is the issue …

   e) There has been a sharp decrease between 1930 and 1950.

   f) The quality of a society depends in the education level.

   g) America had the biggest figure for crime.

3. **Proof-reading a longer text is more difficult.**

   The following was written by a student who was asked to describe his background and future plans.

Underline the errors and then write in suitable corrections.

NB. As the subject is personal, a relatively informal style is acceptable here.

I come from China, which is a very traditional country. I think before give my own situation and plan, I have to say something about my country, because her cultures effect me very much. My country has 5,000 years history, so in my brain there are a lot of thing which is from it.

When I first arrived UK I studied in Cambridge, which is the best university all over the world. Although I just studied in a language school in Cambridge, I felt so good. I learned a lot not only from the school but also from the Cambridge society. That is why I choose Cambridge to learn my foundation course. The foundation course just for oversea studies to improve their English.

I would like to study buiness, because when China join in WTO, my country will need a lot of people who know business very well. So I will choose business foundation course, computer and mathematics, because computer is very useful in modern society. In the future course I think the big problem is vocabulary, so I am planning to remember as many as I can. I will spend more time on mathematics, because I never learn it before.

Another problem is to finish the homework in time. Sometimes I think the homework is no useful for me, so I just leave it, which is a bad customer. The last and the big is homesick, which always slow down my progress, but studying broad is my own choice, I have to try my best.

2. Elements of Writing

Student Introduction

The *Elements of Writing* are the various skills that are needed for most types of academic writing, whether a short report, a longer essay or a dissertation. Many essays, for example, begin by defining a term in the title (Unit 4), then make some generalisations about the subject (Unit 7), before going on to provide examples of the main areas the writer wishes to examine (Unit 6). Throughout the essay the writer needs to provide references to sources used (Unit 9) and to employ an appropriate academic style (Unit 10). Most academic subjects also require discussion of numbers (Unit 8), and graphs and charts (Unit 12). The model essays in Part 4 provide examples of how these various elements are employed in one text (Part 4 Unit 4).

In the case of Units 3 and 5 (*Comparisons* and *Discussion*), students should note that the comparison or discussion might apply to the overall pattern of the essay or to just one section. It is common, for instance, for longer essays to have a discussion section before the conclusion. In either case similar structures can be used.

There is no fixed order for working on the units in *Elements of Writing*. They are organised alphabetically for easy access, but most students will have their own priorities. Business students, for example, might choose to begin by working on *Visual Information* (Unit 12).

1. Cause and Effect

1. **The relationship between two situations can be shown in a variety of ways:**

| CAUSE: heavy rain | ⟶ | EFFECT: flooding |

Heavy rain *causes* flooding.
Heavy rain *leads to* flooding.
Heavy rain *results in* flooding.
Heavy rain *produces* flooding.

| EFFECT: flooding | ⟵ | CAUSE: heavy rain |

cross reference

3.11   Passives

Flooding *is caused by* heavy rain (note use of passive).
Flooding *is produced by* heavy rain.
Flooding *results from* heavy rain.

cross reference

3.5   Conjunctions

2. **It is also possible to use conjunctions that demonstrate cause and effect.**

Cause	Effect
because (of)	so
since	therefore
as	consequently
owing to	which is why
due to	

Because it rained heavily, the flooding was severe. (*because* + verb)
The flooding occurred *because of* days of heavy rain. (*because* + noun)
Owing to the heavy rain the flooding was severe.
It rained heavily for days, *therefore* the flooding was severe. (used in mid-sentence)
NB It is more common to use conjunctions to illustrate particular situations.

3. *Complete the following sentences with a suitable verb or conjunction.*
   a) Childhood vaccination . . . . reduced infant mortality.
   b) . . . . the cold winter hospital admissions increased.
   c) Printing money . . . . higher inflation.
   d) The summer was extremely dry, ... many trees died.
   e) Increased ownership of video recorders . . . . falling cinema attendance.
   Write three more sentences from your own subject area.
   f)
   g)
   h)

4. *Use conjunctions to complete the following paragraph.*

WHY WOMEN LIVE LONGER

Some British scientists now believe that women live longer than men a) ....
T cells, a vital part of the immune system that protects the body from diseases. Previously,
various theories have attempted to explain longer female life expectancy. Biologists claimed that
women lived longer b) ....they need to bring up children. Others argued that
men take more risks, c) ....they die earlier. But a team from Imperial College
think that the difference may be d) ....women having better immune systems.
Having studied a group of men and women they found that the body produces fewer T cells as
it gets older, e) ....the ageing process. However, they admit that this may not be
the only factor, and f) ....another research project may be conducted.

5. *Study the flowchart and complete the paragraph that describes it.*

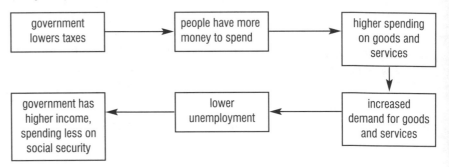

If a country is suffering from economic recession, the government can reduce taxation.

6. *Draw a flowchart similar to the one above, for your own subject, and write a paragraph to describe it.*

2.   Cohesion

3.5 *Conjunctions*

1. **Cohesion means linking phrases together so that the whole text is clear and readable.**

   It is achieved by several methods, such as the use of conjunctions. Another is the linking of phrases and sentences with words like *he, they* and *that* which refer back to something mentioned before:

   Jane Austen wrote six major novels in *her* short life. *They* deal with

   domestic drama in middle-class families.

   Examples of reference words and phrases

pronouns	he/she/it/they
possessive pronouns	his/her/hers/their/theirs
objective pronouns	her/him/them
demonstrative pronouns	this/that/these/those
other phrases	the former/the latter/the first/the second

2. *Read the following paragraph and complete the table.*

   Jenkins (1987) has researched the life cycle *of new businesses*. *He* found that *they* have an *average life of only 4.7 years*. *This* is due to two main reasons; one *economic* and one *social*. *The former* appears to be a lack of capital, *the latter* a failure to carry out sufficient market research. Jenkins considers that together *these* account for approximately 70% of business failures.

Reference	Reference word/phrase
Jenkins	he
new businesses	
average life of only 4.7 years	
one economic	
one social	
the former…, the latter…	

3. *Read the paragraph and complete the table below to show what the reference words (in italic) refer to.*

   There is little prospect of improvement in the standard of living of the villagers from *their* present low level without the support of electricity. Presently, the households can enjoy only a limited number of hours of illumination based on kerosene or diesel. *These* are not cheap and so are not affordable by a large majority of the rural masses. *This* restricts the range as well as the intensity of *their* activities severely. But even if supply of power from *these sources* is available more abundantly, there is the problem of adverse environmental effects of *such use*.

Reference	Reference word
	their
	these
	this
	their
	these sources
	such use

4. *In the following paragraph, insert suitable reference words from the box below in the gaps.*

Disposable razor blades were invented by Gillette at the beginning of the twentieth century. a) ...... were a simple idea but at first b) .... found it very hard to sell c) .... d) .... was because nobody had marketed a throw-away product before. However, e) .... use of advertising to stimulate demand gradually increased sales and before long f) .... became a millionaire.

| he/he/his/them/this/they |

5. *Complete these paragraphs with suitable reference words from the table in (1).*

A) The Victoria and Albert Museum is in South Kensington in London. a) .... is named after Queen Victoria and b) .... husband, Prince Albert. c) ...... was made Queen in 1837, and married d) .... three years later. e) .... had a happy marriage which produced nine children. f) .... life together was quite simple, although g) .... was the queen of the world's most powerful nation. Albert had a serious character, and perhaps h) .... major achievement was to organise the Great Exhibition of 1851, the profits from which helped to build the Museum.

B) One group of commentators have little faith in the ability of food availability to improve child nutrition. a) .... arguments are supported by the fact that over two-thirds of malnourished children live in countries with food supplies adequate for b) .... population's needs. c) .... point to problems of poverty and to non-food factors, such as children's health and the quality of d) .... care. e) .... belief is that both, but especially f) .... (which is increasing in many countries), play a more significant part in malnutrition than is often admitted.

3. Comparisons

1. **The two basic comparative forms are:**

   The Pacific Ocean is *larger* than the Atlantic.

   His work is *more interesting* than hers.

   a) *-er* is added to one-syllable adjectives (*slow/slower*) and two-syllable adjectives ending in *–y* (*easy/easier*).

   b) *more* .... is used with words of two or more syllables:

   careful/more careful

   quickly/more quickly.

   However, there are some two-syllable words that can use either form:

   simple/simpler/more simple.

```
cross reference
```
2.8 Numbers

2. **Comparisons can be made more exact by using** *slightly, considerably* **or** *significantly* **before the comparative:**

   Dickens's novels are *considerably longer* than Austen's.

   The new Mercedes is *slightly more economical* than the old model.

3. *Study the table and complete the exercise below.*

   Cost of sending a letter to a domestic destination (eurocent)

Germany	110
France	85
Japan	62
Britain	60
United States	48
Spain	45

   a) Letters in France are .... in Japan.
   b) Spanish letters are .... German letters.
   c) American letters are .... letters in Britain.
   d) Letters in Germany are .... in America.

4. **The form** *as* .... *as* **can be used to stress similarity:**

   British letters are nearly *as expensive as* Japanese letters.

   It can also be used for quantitative comparison:

   German letters are *twice as expensive as* American letters

   Also: *half as/three times as/*etc.

5. **Note the variety of forms possible:**

   German letters are more expensive than French (ones/letters). (least formal)

   Letters in Germany are more expensive than (those) in France.

The cost of sending a letter is higher in Germany than in France. (most formal)

NB. *high* and *low* are used for comparing abstract concepts such as rates.

Ones can replace the noun when used with an adjective:

German letters are more expensive than Japanese *ones*.

But not in combination with a noun:

Family cars are cheaper than sports cars. (not sports *ones*)

6. *More/less, the most/the least* (followed by adjective), *the most/the fewest* (related to number)

Divorce is *less common* in Greece than in Britain.

The most crowded country in Europe is Holland.

The School of Education offers *the most modules*. (more than others)

7. *Complete the following description of the table in (3) above* (one *word per gap):*

According to the table, Spain is the a) .... expensive country for sending a domestic letter. The USA is b) .... more expensive, while the cost in Britain is c) .... the same d) .... in Japan. France and Germany are the e) .... expensive countries; France being 20% cheaper f) .... Germany. Overall, posting a letter costs g) .... as much in Spain h) .... in Germany.

8. *Study the table and complete the text below* (one *word per gap).*

American spending on leisure activities, 1997, US$ billion

video, audio and computers	80
books and newspapers	51
casino gambling	24
lotteries	18
recorded music	15
theme parks	9
video games	8.5
spectator sports	6
cinema tickets	5.5
racecourse betting	2.5

The table shows that Americans spend the a) .... money ($80 bn.) on video, audio and computer equipment. They spend 40% b) .... on books and newspapers, while casinos, in third place, are c) .... popular d) .... lotteries or recorded music. Americans spend e) .... more on theme parks than f) .... video games, and the cinema, in ninth place, is nearly g) .... popular as spectator sports. The h) .... amount of money is spent on racecourse betting.

cross reference

3.8 Nationality Language

9. *Study the table below and complete the paragraph comparing life expectancy in European countries (**one** word per gap).*

Country	Adult alcohol intake per year, litres	Cigarettes smoked per day per adult	Life expectancy in years – male	Life expectancy in years – female
Austria	11.9	4.6	74.2	80.5
Belgium	11.7	4.3	73.8	80.5
Britain	9.4	4.2	74.3	79.5
Denmark	12.1	4.9	73.1	78.2
Finland	8.4	2.2	73.3	80.3
France	14.1	4.0	74.2	82.1
Germany	11.8	5.0	73.7	80.0
Greece	10.4	8.3	75.1	81.4
Italy	9.4	4.2	74.9	81.3
Norway	4.8	1.7	75.4	81.0
Portugal	13.6	4.6	71.4	78.7
Sweden	6.4	2.4	76.7	81.8
Switzerland	11.8	5.6	76.1	82.2
EU average	11.1	4.5	74.1	80.5

The table a) ....that Swedish men have the b) ....life expectancy in Europe, while women live the c) ....in Switzerland. d) .... average women in Europe live six years longer e) ....men. Men in Portugal have f) ....lowest life expectancy (71.4 years), while the lowest for women is Denmark (78.2 years), which is g) ....less than in Portugal (78.7 years).

10. *Complete the following paragraph comparing cigarette smoking in Europe.*

The table shows considerable variations in cigarette smoking in Europe. The highest rate is ....

11. *Write another paragraph comparing alcohol intake in Europe.*

4.   Definitions

1.13   Introductions

1. **In academic writing, definitions are normally needed in two situations:**
   a) In introductions, to clarify a word or phrase in the title.
   b) More generally, to explain a word or phrase that may be either very technical (and so not in normal dictionaries), or very recent, or with no widely agreed meaning.

Word	Category	Detail	Use
A *lecture*	is a formal talk	given to a large group,	often used for teaching
An *assignment*	is a task	often given to students	for teaching or assessment

2. *Insert suitable category words in the following definitions.*
   a) A *barometer* is a scientific .... designed to measure atmospheric pressure.
   b) *Kidneys* are .... that separate waste fluid from the blood.
   c) A *multi-national company* is a business .... that operates in many countries.
   d) *Reinforced concrete* is a building .... consisting of cement, sand and steel rods.
   e) *Bullying* is a pattern of anti-social .... found in many schools.
   f) *Recycling* is a .... in which materials are used again.
   g) A *recession* is a .... of reduced economic activity.
   h) *Postcodes* are a .... for making mail delivery more efficient.

3. **More complete definitions may be written by adding examples or extra information:**

   A mortgage is a type of loan (that is) used for buying property, in which the lender has the security of the property.

   Complete and extend the following definitions.
   a) Distillation is a .... used to ....
   b) A psychiatrist is a .... who specialises in ....
   c) An MSc. is a.................... awarded on completion of..........................
   d) A trades union is a(n).................... that exists to protect.....................
   e) Malaria is a ....caused by...................................
   f) Wheat is a..............used for...

4. *Study the following examples and underline the term being defined.*
   a) ... the definition for a failed project ... ranges from abandoned projects to projects that simply do not meet their full potential or simply have schedule overrun problems.
   b) Development is a socio-economic–technological process having the main objective of raising the standards of living of the people.

c) Electronic commerce is characterised by an absence of physical proximity between the buyer and seller in conducting the search, assessment and transaction stages of a transaction.

d) Bowlby (1982) suggested that attachment is an organised system whose goal is to make individuals feel safe and secure.

e) … the non-linear effect called 'self-brightening' in which large-amplitude waves decay more slowly than small-amplitude ones.

The examples above illustrate the variety of methods employed in definitions:

(a) gives various examples that fall into the grouping the author wishes to examine.

(b), (d) and (e) use category words: *process, system, effect*.

(c) defines the term in a negative way (*an absence*).

(d) quotes a definition from another writer.

5. **When writing introductions, it is often helpful to define a term in the title, even when it may be in common use, to demonstrate that you have thought about it and that you have a clear idea what it means in your essay.**

   Title: Higher education should be free and open to all – Discuss.

   Higher education in Britain means university-level study for first or higher degrees, normally at the age of 18 or above.

   Study the following titles, decide which term needs defining in each, and write a definition for **two** *of them.*

   a) Compare the murder rate for countries with capital punishment with that for those without it.

   b) The department store is a nineteenth-century creation which has no future in the twenty-first century – Discuss.

   c) The incidence of post-natal depression appears to be rising. What are the most effective methods of treating the condition?

6. *Select several terms from your own subject area and write extensive definitions for them.*

5. Discussion

cross reference

4.5   *Discursive Essay*

1. **Many essay titles require the writer to examine both sides of a case and to conclude by coming down in favour of one side.**

   These may be called **discussion, for and against** or **argument** essays. For example:

   a) School uniforms – a step forward or a step back? – Discuss.

   b) Discuss the advantages and disadvantages of state control of industry.

   Discussion vocabulary

+	–
benefit	drawback
advantage	disadvantage
a positive aspect	a negative feature
pro (informal)	con (informal)
plus (informal)	minus (informal)
one minor *benefit* of school uniforms is ..	a serious *drawback* to state control is …

cross reference

1.12   *Organising the Main Body*

2. **There are two basic outlines for a discussion essay:**

   i) School uniforms?

   a) advantages: reduce social inequality/encourage group identity/avoid choice

   b) disadvantages: loss of individuality/expense/unfashionable

   c) discussion: overall, benefits more valuable in most cases

   ii) School uniforms?

   a) social: emphasises group values – diminishes individual choice

   b) practical: expensive for poor families but easier to get dressed

   c) discussion: overall, benefits more valuable in most cases

3. *Choose one of the titles below and write down as many pros and cons in the box as possible. Then prepare a plan using one of the outlines above.*

   a) Instead of going out to work, mothers should stay at home and look after their children until they are at least five – Discuss.

   b) Fast food, which is spreading round the world and destroying national cultures, should be resisted. To what extent do you agree?

+	–

> Title:
>
> a)
>
> b)
>
> c)
>
> d)

4. **Presenting your case.**

   It is better to use impersonal phrases rather than *I think*:

   It is widely believed that young children need to be with their mothers …

   Most people consider that fast food is very convenient …

   It is generally agreed that school uniforms develop a group identity …

   It is probable/possible that fast food will become more acceptable …

   This evidence suggests that most children benefit from nurseries …

   However, if you want to defend a minority point of view, you can use the following:

   It can be argued that children benefit from a diet of hamburgers.

   It has been suggested that school uniforms make children more rebellious.

   Some people believe that nursery education damages children.

   It is important to show that you are aware of counter-arguments, which can be presented first.

   Study the example and write similar sentences about working mothers and fast food using ideas from (3).

Counter-argument	Your position
Although it has been suggested that school uniforms make children more rebellious,	it is generally agreed that uniforms develop a group identity.

cross reference

1.9   *Combining Sources*
3.16   *Referring Verbs*

5. **Before giving your own opinion, it is necessary to show that you have read the relevant sources and have studied the evidence.**

   Opinions without evidence have little value. The following paragraph discusses the environmental effects of deforestation.

   Lomborg (2001) *claims* that the danger of extinction of species has been exaggerated. He says that the number of species had been expected to decline dramatically within the next half century, but *maintains* that this is unlikely: 'Species … seem more resilient than expected.' He *points out* that in the eastern USA, although 98% of the original forests have been cleared, only one forest bird became extinct in the process. Against this, Brooks (2001) *feels* that Lomborg is ignoring the true rate of forest loss and the related extinction of species: 'The ongoing wave of extinctions, due primarily to deforestation in the moist tropics, has been widely documented.' It *seems* that Lomborg, as a statistician, is too dependent on optimistic data, and is ignoring the widespread concerns of wildlife experts.

The paragraph has the following structure:

> Lomborg – paraphrase + quotation
>
> Brooks – paraphrase + quotation
>
> Writer's comment on Lomborg + opinion

6. *Complete the following paragraph, which discusses air pollution, to give an opinion.*

According to Lomborg (2001), air quality is improving in rich countries. He gives the example of London, where he claims that the air is cleaner now than it has been since 1585, thanks to decreases in smoke and sulphur dioxide. Brooks (2001), however, argues that Lomborg is 'ignoring the more recent global rise in toxic contaminants, now found at high concentrations … even in the remote reaches of the Arctic.' It appears that ....
....
....
....

7. *List in the box as many ideas as possible for and against the following subject:*

'Civilisation began in the city, and the city remains the only place for civilised people to live' – Discuss.

+	–

8. *Prepare a plan for this title, using one of the outlines in (2) above.*
   a)
   b)
   c)
   d)

9. *Write an essay on this title, making use of phrases from (4) above.*

6.   Examples

1. **When writing essays it is often better to support statements by giving examples.**

   Compare the following:

   a) Many plants and animals are threatened by global warming.

   b) Many plants and animals are threatened by global warming. In southern Britain, *for example*, the beech tree may become extinct within 30 years.

   The second sentence provides concrete details of a plant species, an area and a time scale to support the main statement.

cross reference

3.5 *Conjunctions*

2. **Phrases for introducing examples include:**

   Many departments, *for instance/for example* engineering, now offer foundation courses. (note use of commas)

   A few courses *such as*/e.g. MBA require work experience.

   Many universities, *particularly/especially* UK ones, ask overseas students for IELTS scores. (note the focus)

   Some subjects are heavily oversubscribed. *A case in point* is medicine. (for single examples)

   Use suitable example phrases to complete the following sentences.

   a) As the climate warms, wetland species .... frogs may find their habitat reduced.

   b) Some animals can migrate to cooler areas. .... are birds, which can move easily.

   c) Many plants, trees ...., will find it difficult to move to wetter regions in the north.

   d) Certain reptiles, ... snakes, may benefit from drier and warmer summers.

   e) Rising sea levels may bring some advantages .... expanding wetland areas.

3. *Find a suitable example for each sentence.*

   Example:

   Various sectors in the economy are experiencing labour shortages.

   Various sectors in the economy, *for instance engineering*, are experiencing labour shortages.

   a) A number of sports have become very profitable due to the sale of television rights.

   b) Some British universities offer special courses in English for overseas students.

   c) In recent years many women have made significant contributions to the political world.

   d) Three-year guarantees are now being offered by most car makers.

   e) Certain diseases are proving much harder to combat than was expected 20 years ago.

f) Many musical instruments use strings to make music.

g) Several mammals are currently in danger of extinction.

4. *Provide examples in the following paragraph where they appear necessary.*

Students who go to study abroad often experience a type of culture shock when they arrive in the new country. Customs which they took for granted in their own society are not followed in the host country. Even everyday patterns of life may be different. When these are added to the inevitable differences which occur in every country students may at first feel confused. They may experience rapid changes of mood, or even want to return home. However, most soon make new friends and, in a relatively short period, are able to adjust to their new environment. They may even find that they prefer some aspects of their new surroundings, and forget that they are not at home for a while!

5. Another small group of phrases is used when there is only one example. This is a kind of restatement:

The world's biggest software company, *i.e.* Microsoft, is buying a share of the cable business.

> in other words/namely/that is to say/i.e./viz. (in very formal English only)

In the following sentences, add a suitable phrase from the box below.

a) His mother's sister was a small but very remarkable woman.

b) When the liquid reached boiling point the reaction began.

c) All the plants and animals at risk in the region must be protected.

d) At this stage, all the students should be rigorously evaluated.

e) It was cold, wet and windy.

> namely 140 degrees
> in other words, an English summer's day
> i.e. his aunt
> viz., given an examination
> that is to say, the endangered wildlife
> namely, the Atlantic Ocean

7. Generalisations

1. *Decide if you agree with the following:*

   a) When two Englishmen meet, their first talk is of the weather. (Samuel Johnson)

   b) A bank is a place that will lend you money if you can prove that you don't need it. (Bob Hope)

   The above are well-known quotations, which are remembered because they are funny, though only partly true. This shows that generalisations are easy to remember, if not always accurate.

2. **In written work generalisations are very useful because they can be used to present complex ideas or data in a simple form:**

   Large companies can offer better career opportunities.

   Language is an important means of communication.

   Study the table below and compare the statements.

   UK smokers by gender

Men	Women
43.8%	56.2%

   a) 56.2 % of British smokers are women.

   b) The majority of British smokers are women.

   The first sentence is more accurate, but the second, which contains a generalisation, is easier to understand. However, using generalisations does involve a loss of precision, so the writer must judge when they can be used safely, and when it is better to give the full data.

cross reference

3.4   *Caution*

3. **There are two ways of making a generalisation:**

   a) Using the plural: *Computers are useful machines.*

   b) Using definite article and the singular: *The computer is a useful machine.* (less common/more formal)

   It is better to avoid absolute phrases such as *cats are cleverer than dogs.* Instead use more cautious phrases such as *cats tend to be cleverer than dogs* or *most cats are more intelligent than dogs.*

   Write generalisations on the following topics.

   a) child/noise   Example: *Children are often noisy.*

   b) flowers/presents ....

   c) city/pollution ....

   d) fresh fruit/health ....

   e) television/important ....

4. *Read the following text and underline the generalisations.*

   Li Pang is a Chinese student studying architecture in Manchester. He enjoys the style of teaching as well as the cosmopolitan lifestyle the city provides. Many international students attend British universities. Most welcome the chance to meet classmates from all over the world, and all are pleased to have the chance to improve their English. When he goes home to Shanghai, Li Pang will have a network of international contacts to support his future career.

2.3 *Comparisons*
2.8 *Numbers*

5. *Study the table.*

Britain	1979	1989	1999
inflation rate	13.4%	7.8%	3.4%
interest rate	12%	13.7%	5.5%
unemployment	4.1%	6.1%	4.6%
average income	£5,000	£11,700	£19,000
average house price	£19,800	£61,500	£68,300

When making generalisations it is easy to over-generalise, using inadequate data.

The following statements were written using the data in the table above, but each contains an error. Find the error and re-write the sentence.

Example:

People were much richer in 1999 than 20 years earlier.

This ignores inflation over the period. It is more accurate to say:

Average incomes in 1999 were nearly four times higher than in 1979.

a) Between 1979 and 1999, the worst period for unemployment was 1989.

b) Inflation fell steadily for 20 years after 1979.

c) There was a dramatic rise in house prices in these two decades.

d) Interest rates peaked in 1989.

6. *Study the table below and complete the generalisations.*

Regional population in 2000 and forecasts for 2100, with percentage over 60 years old (millions)

Region	2000	% over 60	2100	% over 60
N. America	314	16	454	40
W. Europe	456	20	392	45
S. Asia	1,367	7	1,958	35
S. America	515	8	934	33
N. Africa	173	6	333	32

   a) By 2100, nearly half the population of W. Europe may......................... .

   b) The population of N. Africa may.. .

   c) S. Asia and S. America both have.. .

   d) W. Europe is likely to experience a... .

   e) By 2100, all these regions may... .

7. *Read this text about dreams and write five generalisations using the data.*

A recent survey on dreams, completed by over 10,000 people, found that 68% of all dreams came into the 'anxiety' category. Being chased was the most common dream, recorded by 72%. Dreams about falling (which signify insecurity) are also very common, being recorded by 70%.

55% have dreamed about relatives and friends who have died. Many people believe that dreams can foretell the future, but only 42% have experienced this type. 28% of those surveyed have dreams about food, which seem to occur during periods of weight watching, but 23% have been pleased by dreams of finding money.

Example:

Anxiety seems to be the cause of most dreams.

   a) ....

   b) ....

   c) ....

   d) ....

   e) ....

8.   Numbers

1. **Discussing statistical data is a necessary part of much academic writing:**

   Approximately 1800 children between the ages of 5 and 12 years were randomly selected.

   Already 3% of the US working population (1.55 million) are employed in 70,000 centres ...

   The earth's atmosphere appears to be gaining 3.3 billion metric tons of carbon annually ...

   ... but 5 winters in the 20th century were more than 2.4°C colder than average.

   Figures and **numbers** are both used to talk about statistical data in a general sense.

   > The *figures* in the report need to be read critically.

   Digits are individual numbers. Both **fractions** (½) and **decimals** (0.975) may be used.

   > 4,539 – a four *digit* number
   >
   > £225,000 – a six *figure* salary (a number)

   Figure (*Fig*) 3 – Infant mortality rates in twelfth-century France (a diagram)

   no final -*s* on *hundred/thousand/million*:

   > Six *million* people live in the region.
   >
   > but: *Thousands* died in the last outbreak of cholera.

2. **When presenting data, the writer must attempt to be accurate without confusing the reader with too much detail.**

   In some cases, where the actual number is unimportant, words or phrases may replace numbers to simplify the text:

   > *43* villages were cut off by the heavy snowstorm.
   >
   > *Dozens of* villages were cut off by the heavy snowstorm.

   The following words or phrases can be used to describe quantity.

   > *Few* students attended her lecture. (less than expected)
   >
   > *Several* bodies have been discovered under the temple floor. (3–4)
   >
   > *Various* attempts were made to reach the sunken ship. (3–6)
   >
   > *Dozens of* politicians attended the opening ceremony. (30–60)
   >
   > *Scores of* books are published every week. (50–100).

   Re-write the following sentences using one of the words or phrases above.

   a) Only four people responded to the questionnaire.

   b) They received nearly 100 applications for the post.

   c) She made five or six proposals to improve the team's performance.

   d) He found over 50 factual errors in the article.

   e) They made three or four drafts before writing the final report.

cross reference

2.12   *Visual Information*

3. Percentages are commonly used for expressing rates of change:

Overseas students in the university 1997–2000

1997	1998	1999	2000
200	300	600	1000

Between 1997 and 1998, the number of overseas students increased by 50%.
The number increased by 100% the following year.
There was a 400% increase between 1997 and 2000.

4. *Study the following expressions, which are also used to simplify statistics.*

one in three	a third/a quarter
twice/three times as many	the majority/the minority
a tenfold increase	fifty per cent, a percentage
to double/to halve	on average/the average number
the most/the least	a small/large proportion

Rewrite each sentence in a simpler way, using one of the expressions above.

a) Of the 415 people interviewed, 308 said that they supported the president.

b) Last year the number of students on the course was 28, the year before it was 20 and this year it is 24.

c) In 1965 a litre of petrol cost 10p, while the price is now 80p.

d) Out of 18 students in the group, 12 were women.

e) The new type of train reduced the journey time to Madrid from seven hours to three hours 20 minutes.

f) 15 of the students studied law, eight finance and three engineering.

g) The numbers applying to this department have risen from 350 last year to 525 this year.

5. *Re-write the following sentences to present the data in a simpler way.*

   a) The population of the European part of the former Soviet Union is declining rapidly. It is forecast to fall by 18 m to 220 m in 2025, and to drop to 140 m by 2100.

   Example:

   The population of the European part of the former Soviet Union is forecast to fall by nearly 10% by 2025, and by nearly 40% by the end of the century.

   b) The numbers of visitors to the temples show a remarkable pattern. In 1998 just 40,000 made the journey, 83,000 in 1999 and 171,000 in 2000.

   c) More than 80% of British students complete their first degree course; in Italy the figure is 35%.

   d) Tap water costs 0.07p per litre while bottled water, on average, costs 50p per litre.

   e) Only 8% of the women surveyed believed that they had the same rights as men. A considerable 37% complained that they had far fewer rights.

   f) Life expectancy for men in the UK rose from 49 to 74 during the twentieth century.

   g) The same operation cost £1,850 at a hospital in Blackburn, £2,400 in Birmingham and £2,535 in London.

   h) In 1086 about 15% of England was forested, compared with only 4.8% in 1870.

9.   References and Quotations

1. **A reference is an acknowledgement that you are making use of another writer's ideas or data in your writing:**

   As Donner (1997) pointed out, low inflation does not always lead to low interest rates.

   There are three main reasons for giving references:

   a) To avoid the charge of **plagiarism**, which is using another person's ideas or research without acknowledgement.

   b) The reference can give more authority to your writing, for it shows you are familiar with other research on the topic.

   c) The reader can find the original source by using the reference section, which would list the full publishing details of Donner's book:

   Donner, F. (1997) *Macroeconomics.* Borchester: Borchester University Press

2. *Decide which of the following need references.*

   a) A mention of facts or figures from another writer

   b) An idea of your own

   c) Some data you have found from your own research

   d) A theory suggested by another researcher

   e) A quotation from a work by any author

   f) Something that is agreed to be common knowledge

1.6   Note-Making

3. **In order to give references accurately it is important to follow the following procedure:**

   a) When reading and note-making, keep a careful record of the details of your sources. For a long piece of writing such as a dissertation a card index is useful.

   b) Find out which system of referencing is used in your subject area. You can do this by studying current textbooks and journals and checking departmental guidelines.

   c) Follow one of the methods illustrated below to give the reference.

4. a) **Summary of a writer's ideas.**

   Orwell (1940) pointed out that although Charles Dickens described eating large meals in many of his books, he never wrote about farming. He explains this contradiction in terms of Dickens' upbringing in London, remote from the countryside.

   b) **Quotation of a writer's words.**

   Orwell clearly highlighted this inconsistency in Dickens: 'It is not merely a coincidence that Dickens never writes about agriculture and writes endlessly about food. He was a Cockney, and London is the centre of the earth in rather the same sense that the belly is the centre of the body.' (Orwell, 1940: pp. 53-54)

   c) **Mixture of summary and quotation.**

   As Orwell (1940) noted, Dickens frequently described food but was uninterested in food production. He considered that this was because of the writer's background: 'He was a Cockney, and London is the centre of the earth.'(pp.53–54)

5. *Read the following extract from the same essay* ('Charles Dickens' in *Inside the Whale*, **Orwell, G., 1940: pp.54–55**)

What he does not noticeably write about, however, is *work*. In Dickens' novels anything in the nature of work happens off-stage. The only one of his heroes who has a plausible profession is David Copperfield, who is first a shorthand writer and then a novelist, like Dickens himself. With most of the others, the way they earn their living is very much in the background.

   a) *Write a summary of the author's ideas, including a suitable reference.*

   b) *Introduce a quotation of the key part of the extract, again referring to the source.*

   Combine (a) and (b), again acknowledging the source.

| cross reference |

3.16   Referring Verbs

6. **Referring verbs use both the present and the past tenses.**

   It is probably best to use the present tense for recent sources or when you feel that the ideas or data are still valid:

   Rathbone (1997) demonstrates the limitations of video-conferencing.

   The past tense suggests that the source is older and the ideas perhaps out-of-date:

   Steinbeck (1965) explored a link between cancer and diet.

7. **There are three main systems of reference in use in academic writing:**

   a) The system illustrated above (the Harvard) is the most common. Note the following:

   Hunter (1989) states … (date of publication in brackets when referring verb is used)

   Women pose less security risk. (Burke and Pollock, 1993) (authors and date in brackets after summary)

   NB. For quotations page numbers should also be given after the date. Details of the organisation of the reference section are given in (8) below.

   b) Numbers in brackets are inserted in the text for each source, and at the end of the chapter or article the references are listed in number order:

   A survey of Fortune 500 companies found that over 70% have problems recruiting skilled staff (1). Some analysts argue that this could be as high as 90% (2).

   1. Cuervo, D. 1990, Whither Recruitment? *HR Journal* **13**. pp. 23–39.

   2. Segall, N. 1996, *Cross-cultural studies*, Harper & Row, New York pp. 173-4.

   c) A third system uses footnotes:

   More than 80% of families own or are buying their own homes.[2]

   In this system the references are listed at the bottom of the page:

   2. *The Economist*, 13 January 1996, pp. 27–8.

   NB. A full reference section is required at the end of the article or book.

8. **Organising the bibliography/references**

   Here is the reference section of an essay written by a business student.

   Study the pattern of organisation and answer the following questions.

a) How are the entries ordered?

b) What is the difference between the information provided for:
   i) a book by one author
   ii) an edited book
   iii) a source on the internet
   iv) an article in a journal

c) When are *italics* used?

d) How are capital letters used in titles?

e) How is a source with no given author listed?

REFERENCES

1. Brzeski, W. (1999) *The Polish Housing Market* www.onenet.pl (Access date 15 Feb. 2000).

2. Hill, S. (1989) *Managerial Economics, The Analysis of Business Decisions.* London: Macmillan Education Ltd. pp. 100–135.

3. Koutsoyiannis, A.P. (1963) 'Demand function for tobacco' in Wagner, L. (ed) *Readings in Applied Microeconomics*. Oxford: Oxford University Press.

4. Mintel Database (2000), *Retail Coffee Market in the UK* (31 Jan. 2000) Available via Warwick University Library (Access date 20 Feb. 2000).

5. Pass, C. and Lowes, B. (1997) *Business and Microeconomics*. London: Routledge pp. 16-40.

6. Peck, S. (2000) *Managerial Economics Course Notes*. Warwick Business School.

7. Russell, T. (1995) 'A future for coffee?' *Journal of Applied Marketing* **6** pp. 14–17.

> **Referencing is a complex subject and students are advised to seek specialist advice, e.g. from a library, when referencing less usual sources.**

10. Style

1. *Study the style of this paragraph and underline any examples of poor style.*

   A lot of people think that the weather is getting worse. They say that this has been going on for quite a long time. I think that they are quite right. Research has shown that we now get storms etc all the time.

2. **Academic writing attempts to be precise, semi-formal, impersonal and objective.**

   This does not mean that pronouns like *I* and *we* are never used, but in general the focus is on presenting information as clearly and accurately as possible. In this way such writing differs from normal speech and writing, which is more personal and uses more lively idioms and phrases. Using these guidelines, the paragraph above can be analysed:

A lot of people think…	Imprecise – how many is *a lot*?
…the weather …	Imprecise – *weather* is short-term
…getting worse …	Informal
They say…	Use of pronoun informal
…going on …	Informal phrasal verb
… quite a long time.	Imprecise – how long is this?
I think…	Informal, personal phrase
Research…	Vague – whose research?
…we now get …	Informal
…storms etc …	Vague
…all the time.	Over-generalised

   The paragraph can be rewritten:

   It is widely believed that the climate is deteriorating. It is claimed that this process has been continuing for nearly 100 years. This belief appears to be supported by McKinley (1997), who shows a 55% increase in the frequency of severe winter gales since 1905.

3. **It is difficult to give rules for academic style which apply to all subject areas.**

   When reading books and journals in your area you should note what is acceptable. You will probably meet exceptions to the points below as you read, but if you follow these guidelines you should be able to develop a suitable style of your own.

   a) Do not use idiomatic or colloquial vocabulary: *dad, guy*. Use standard English: *father, man*.

   b) Use vocabulary accurately. There is a difference between *rule* and *law*, or *currency* and *money*, which you are expected to know.

   c) Be as precise as possible when dealing with facts or figures. Avoid phrases such as *about a hundred* or *hundreds of years ago*. If it is necessary to estimate numbers use *approximately* rather than *about*.

cross reference

3.4   *Caution*

cross reference

3.2   *Adverbs*

cross reference

3.11   *Passives*

d) Conclusions should use tentative language. Avoid absolute statements such as *education reduces crime*. Instead use cautious phrases: *may reduce crime* or *tends to reduce crime*.

e) Avoid adverbs that show your personal attitude: *luckily, remarkably, surprisingly*.

f) Do not contract verb forms: *don't, can't*. Use the full form: *do not, cannot*.

g) Although academic English tends to use the passive more than standard English, it should not be over-used. Both have their place. Compare:

Manners (1995) claims that most companies perform worse when ...

It is widely agreed that most companies perform worse when ...

In the first case, the focus is on the source, in the second on what companies do.

h) Avoid the following:

like for introducing examples. Use *such as* or *for instance*.

thing and combinations: *nothing* or *something*. Use *factor, issue* or *topic*.

lots of. Use *a significant/considerable number*.

little/big. Use *small/large*.

get phrases such as *get better/worse*. Use *improve* and *deteriorate*.

i) Do not use question forms such as *What were the reasons for the decline in wool exports?* Instead use statements: *There were four main reasons for the decline…*

j) Avoid numbering sections of your text, except in certain reports. Use conjunctions and signposting expressions to introduce new sections (*Turning to the question of taxation …*). Sub-headings are widely used.

k) When writing lists, avoid using *etc.* or *and so on*. Insert *and* before the last item:

The forests of the twelfth century consisted of oak, ash and lime.

cross reference

3.6   *Formality in Verbs*

l) Avoid using two-word verbs such as *go on* or *bring up* if there is a suitable synonym. Use *continue* or *raise*.

4. *In the following, first underline the examples of poor style and then re-write them in a more suitable way:*

a) Lots of people think that the railways are getting worse.

b) Sadly, serious crime like murder is going up.

c) You can't always trust the numbers in that report.

d) The second thing is that most kids in that district will become criminals.

e)   I think that there's a big risk of more strikes, disorder etc.

f)   A few years ago they allowed women to vote.

g)   Regrettably, the inflation in Russia led to increased poverty, illness and so on.

h)   Sometime soon they will find a vaccine for malaria.

i)   What were the main causes of the American Revolution?

5.   *Re-write the following paragraphs in better style.*

a)   These days a lot of kids are starting school early. Years ago, they began at five, but now it's normal to start at four or younger. Why is this? One thing is that mums need to get back to work. Is it good for the kids? Jenkins has studied this and says that early schooling causes social problems like stealing, drug-taking etc. I think he's right and we should pay mums to stay at home.

b)   Why are there so many jams on the roads these days? One thing is that public transport like trains, buses etc is so dear. A long time ago cars cost a lot but now, unfortunately, they've got a lot cheaper. Another thing is that driving is a lot nicer than waiting for a bus. The trouble is that if everyone buys a car the roads get packed.

11. Synonyms

cross reference

1.7 Paraphrasing

1. When writing it is necessary to find synonyms in order to provide variety and interest for the reader:

General Motors is the *largest motor company in the world*, with total revenues amounting to 15% of the *global automotive* market. *The giant firm* employs 360,000 people *internationally*.

largest company	giant firm
motor	automotive
in the world	global/internationally

Synonyms are not always exactly the same in meaning, but it is important not to change the register. *Firm* is a good synonym for *company*, but *boss* is too informal to use for *manager*.

2. a) The accuracy of a synonym is often dependent on context. Both *pupil* and *student* could be used to identify a 15-year-old schoolgirl, but when she goes to university only *student* is normally used. *Scholar* might be a possible synonym, but it is very formal. Similarly, at university a *lecturer* could also be called a *teacher*, but in school the only possible synonym for *teacher* is the old-fashioned *master* or *mistress*.

b) Many basic words, e.g. *culture, economy, society* or *science*, have no effective synonyms.

cross reference

3.14 Prepositions after Verbs

3. Some common academic synonyms.

Nouns		Verbs	
goal	target	reduce	decrease
study	research	achieve	reach
results	findings	alter	change
area	field	evaluate	examine
authority	source	claim	suggest
benefit	advantage	assist	help
category	type	attach	join
component	part	challenge	question
concept	idea	clarify	explain
behaviour	conduct	collapse	fall down
controversy	argument	concentrate	focus
feeling	emotion	confine	limit
beliefs	ethics	show	demonstrate
expansion	increase	eliminate	remove
interpretation	explanation	found	establish

▶

issue	topic	develop	evolve
method	system	maintain	insist
option	possibility	predict	forecast
statistics	figures	prohibit	ban
framework	structure	retain	keep
trend	tendency	strengthen	reinforce
		accelerate	speed up

4. *Find synonyms for the words and phrases in italic.*

   a) Professor Hicks *questioned* the *findings* of the *research*.

   b) The *statistics show* a steady *expansion* in applications.

   c) The institute's *prediction* has caused a major *controversy*.

   d) Cost seems to be the *leading drawback* to that *system*.

   e) They will *concentrate* on the first *option*.

   f) After the lecture she tried to *clarify* her *concept*.

   g) Three *issues* need to be *examined*.

   h) The *framework* can be *retained* but the *goal* needs to be *altered*.

   i) OPEC, the oil producers' cartel, is to *cut production* to *raise* global prices.

   j) The *trend* to smaller families has *speeded up* in the last decade.

5. *In the following text, replace all the words or phrases in italic with suitable synonyms.*

   A leading French company has started a new programme to reduce costs. The *company's programme* aims to *reduce costs* by $100 million. All the staff have taken pay cuts, and *senior staff* will have their *pay cut* by 20%. The company *aims* to increase profits by 35% next year, and promises that *pay* will be *increased* if that happens.

6. *Identify the synonyms in this text by underlining them and linking them to the word they are substituting for.*

   Example: *agency – organisation*

   The chairman of the UK's food standards *agency* has said that a national advertising campaign is necessary to raise low levels of personal hygiene. The *organisation* is planning a £3m publicity programme to improve British eating habits. A survey has shown that half the population do not wash before eating, and one in five fail to wash before preparing food. There are over 6 million cases of food poisoning in this country every year, and the advertising blitz aims to cut this by 20%. This reduction, the food body believes, could be achieved by regular hand washing prior to meals.

12. Visual Information

1. **Visual devices such as graphs and tables are convenient ways of displaying large quantities of information in a form that is quick and simple to understand.**

   Below are illustrations of some of the main types of visuals used in academic texts. Match the uses (a–f) to the types (1–6) and the examples (A–F) in the box below.

   Uses a) location   b) comparison   c) proportion
         d) function   e) changes in time   f) statistical display

Types	Uses	Example
1. diagram		
2. table		
3. map		
4. pie chart		
5. bar chart		
6. lIne graph		

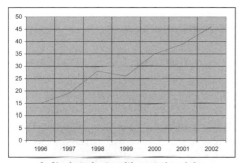

A. % of students with part-time jobs

B. Part-time student enrolments

Business	205
Education	176
History	83
Law	15
Agriculture	7

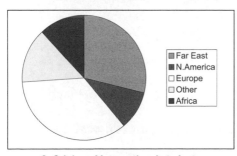

C. Origins of international students

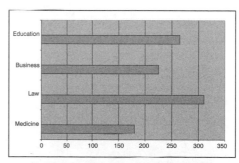

D. Student admissions by subject/2002

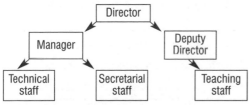

E. Structure of the Language Centre

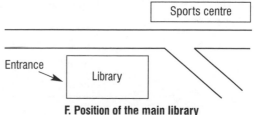

F. Position of the main library

2. The language of change

Verb ⟶	Adverb	Verb ⟶	Adjective + noun
grew	slightly	dropped	a slight drop
rose	gradually	fell	a gradual fall
increased	steadily	decreased	a sharp decrease
climbed	sharply		

Study the graph below and complete the description with phrases from the table above.

Sports centre membership a) .... in 1992, and then
b) .... until 1995, reaching a peak of 4900.
It c) .... in 1996, but d)..................................... the next
year. In 1998 there was a e) ...., then a peak of 6,700 in 1999,
followed by a f) ....in 2000.

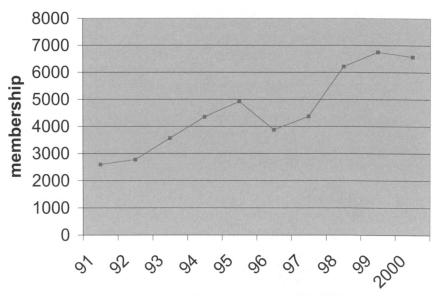

Sports Centre membership 1991–2000

cross reference

2.8 Numbers

3. Although visuals do largely speak for themselves, it is usual to help the reader interpret them by briefly commenting on their main features.

The graph	shows	the changes in the price of oil since 1990
The map	illustrates	the main squatter housing areas in Ankara
The diagram	displays	the experimental set-up of the laboratory study

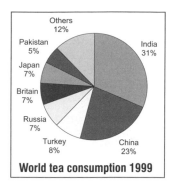

World tea consumption 1999

Read the following descriptions of the chart opposite. Which is better?

a)   The chart shows the quantity of tea consumed by the world's leading tea-consuming nations. India and China together consume more than half the world's tea production, with India alone consuming about one-third. Other significant tea consumers are Turkey, Russia and Britain. 'Others' includes the United States, Iran and Egypt.

b)   The chart shows that 31% of the world's tea is consumed by India, 23% by China, and 8% by Turkey. The fourth largest consumers are Russia, Japan and Britain, with 7% each, while Pakistan consumes 5%. Other countries account for the remaining 12%.

4.   *Complete the following description of the chart below.*

The chart shows population a) .... in a variety of countries around the world.
It b) .... the extreme contrast c) .... crowded nations such as South Korea
(475 people per sq. km.) and much d) .... countries such as Canada (3 people per
sq. km.). Clearly, climate plays a major e) .... in determining population density,
f) .... the least crowded nations g) .... to have extreme climates (e.g. cold
in Russia or dry in Algeria).

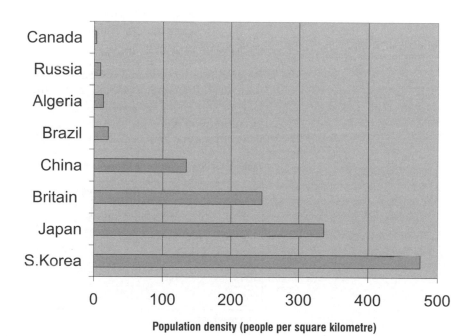

Population density (people per square kilometre)

5. *Complete the following description of the table below.*

Marriage and divorce rates (per 1,000 population)

Country	Marriage rate	Divorce rate
Britain	10.7	3.4
United States	8.6	4.7
Turkey	8.0	0.5
Iran	7.8	0.5
Japan	6.2	1.8
Russia	5.2	3.2
Spain	5.2	0.8
South Africa	4.0	0.9

The a) .... shows the wide variations in marriage and divorce rates in a
b) .... of countries. The c) .... rate varies from 10.7 per thousand in
d) .... to 4.0 in South Africa, while the divorce e) .... ranges from 4.7 in the
United States to 0.5 in Turkey and f) .... It appears that in the United States more than
g) .... of all marriages end in divorce, while in Turkey the
h) .... is less than 10%. This suggests that in countries such as the United States and
Britain the high marriage rate may be a i) .... of the high divorce rate.

6. When referring to visual information in the text, the word *figure* is used for everything (such as maps, charts and graphs) except tables.

Figures and tables should be numbered and given a title. Titles of tables are written above, whereas titles of figures are written below the data. As with other data, sources must be given for all visual information.

Table 4: Gender balance in the School of Computing 1996–2000

Year	Men	Women
1996	109	34
1997	112	45
1998	125	41
1999	108	56
2000	118	72

Source: Author

If you are writing a lengthy work, such as a dissertation, you will need to provide lists of tables and figures, showing numbers, titles and page numbers, after the contents page.

7. *Complete the description of the table above.*

Table 4 shows ....

3. Accuracy in Writing

Student Introduction

Accuracy is only one aspect of the total fabric of good writing. Few teachers will be concerned by one minor mistake with a preposition or a plural in a sentence. But if a student is making mistakes in every other word there is likely to be serious loss of meaning, and their teacher may be unable to mark the work fairly. Many of the most common errors are highlighted in Part 1 Unit 16 (*Proof-Reading*).

Non-native speakers of English tend to have problems of accuracy which relate to their mother tongue. Japanese speakers, for example, find it difficult to use articles because these are not found in Japanese. It is clearly unrealistic for such students to aim at 100% accuracy in their written work, but equally it is important to aim to improve accuracy in order to compete with native-speaker classmates.

The components of *Accuracy in Writing* have been chosen on the basis that they regularly cause difficulties and confusion in students' writing. These units are not intended to replace a standard grammar reference book; instead they assume a good basic knowledge of English grammar and focus on those areas of concern to the writer, rather than the speaker, of English.

As in Part 2, the units are arranged alphabetically. Students may already be aware of their weaknesses and want to focus on the relevant units, or they may seek specific assistance after getting feedback on an essay. There are also two tests of accuracy in the *Writing Tests* which students can use to pinpoint their weak areas.

1.   Abbreviations

1. Abbreviations are an important and expanding feature of contemporary English.

They are used for convenience, and familiarity with abbreviations makes both academic reading and writing easier. Three main types can be found:

a) shortened words – *photo* (*photograph*)

b) acronyms – *UNESCO*

c) others – *NB*

2. Shortened words are often used without the writer being aware of the original form.

Bus comes from *omnibus*, which is never used in modern English, but *refrigerator* is still better in written English than the informal *fridge*. *Public house* is now very formal (*pub* is acceptable), but *television* should be used instead of the idiomatic *telly*.

3. Acronyms are made up of the initial letters of a name or phrase.

For example, *AIDS = acquired immune deficiency syndrome*. They are read as words. The more official acronyms are written in capitals (*NATO*), but others use lower case (*yuppie*). *NATO* stands for *North Atlantic Treaty Organisation*, which is a real body, whereas *yuppie* means *young upwardly mobile professional*, which is a concept.

4. Other abbreviations are read as sets of individual letters.

They include names of countries, organisations and companies (*USA / BBC / IBM*), and also abbreviations that are found only in written English (*PTO = please turn over / Rd = road*).

5. All academic subjects employ abbreviations to save time.

Examples from business/economics include:

GDP = gross domestic product

PR = public relations

PLC = public limited company

CEO = chief executive officer

IMF = International Monetary Fund

WTO = World Trade Organisation

6. There are many standard abbreviations found in some types of writing which have a full stop after them to indicate a shortened form.

For example, *St. = Saint*. Other examples are *govt.* (*government*), *co.* (*company*) and *Oct.* (*October*). With type (b) and (c) abbreviations there is no standard pattern for using full stops, so both *BBC* and *B.B.C.* are used. There is, however, a trend to use full stops less. The important thing is to employ a consistent style in your work.

7. **Abbreviations can be confusing.**

PC, for example, can mean *Police Constable* (in Britain), *personal computer* and also *politically correct*. *CD* may stand for *compact disc* or *corps diplomatique*. *PM* could be *Prime Minister* or *post meridiem*. It is useful to be aware of these potential confusions.

8. **Certain abbreviations are found in all types of academic writing.**

They include:

cf. = compare

e.g. = for example

et al. = and others (used in giving names of multiple authors)

Fig. = figure (for labelling charts and graphs)

ibid. = in the same place (to refer to source mentioned immediately before)

i.e. = that is

K = thousand

op. cit. = in the source mentioned previously

p.a. = yearly

pp. = pages

re = with reference to

9. **Other abbreviations are very subject specific and may be special to one article.**

In that case they need explaining:

… the developing countries with the highest per-capita dietary energy supplies (DES)

… one delegate expressed surprise that Call Centres (CCs) should …

10. *Explain the abbreviations in the following sentences.*

   a) The PM told MPs that the NHS needed reform.

   b) The failure rate among IT projects reaches 70% (Smith et al., 1997).

   c) The world's most populous country i.e. China has joined the WTO.

   d) NB. CVs must be no longer than 3 sides of A4.

   e) See the OECD's recent report on the UK.

   f) The EU hopes to achieve a standard rate of VAT.

   g) The CEO intends to raise spending on R&D by 40%.

   h) Fig.4. Trade patterns on the w.w.w. (1997–2001).

   i) The WHO is concerned about the spread of TB.

   j) Director of PR required – salary approx. $45K.

   k) GM technology is leading to advances in many fields, e.g. forestry.

   l) Prof. Wren claimed that the quality of M.Phil. and Ph.D. research was falling.

2. Adverbs

1. **Adverbs are used in academic texts in a variety of ways.**

   Among the most important are:

   a) to provide more detail, with verbs and adjectives:

   Reasonably good data are available for only …

   … decomposition *eventually* ceases in modern landfills …

   b) individually, often at the beginning of sentences, to introduce new points:

   Currently, the Earth's atmosphere appears to be …

   Alternatively, the use of non-conventional renewable energies …

   NB. These can be similar in function to conjunctions.

2. **Adverbs linked to verbs and adjectives usually fall into three groups.**

   a) Time (when?)

   previously published

   retrospectively examined

   b) Degree (how much?)

   declined *considerably*

   contribute *substantially*

   c) Manner (in what way?)

   medically complicated

   remotely located

cross reference

2.10 Style

3. **Adverbs used individually need to be employed with care.**

   It is dangerous to over-use them, for they may convey a sense of the author's voice commenting on the topic. As the academic writer aims to be objective, adverbs like *fortunately* or *remarkably* may be unsuitable. However, other, less subjective adverbs can be useful for opening paragraphs or linking ideas. The following examples are often followed by a comma.

Time	Relating ideas
recently	clearly
increasingly	obviously
originally	(not) surprisingly
presently	alternatively
currently	similarly
traditionally	(more) importantly

4. *Insert a suitable adverb from the table into the gaps in the sentences.*

   a) Most houses do not have electricity. ……………, then, there is little chance of improving living standards.

b) ...., the internet was mainly used for academic purposes.

c) Some courses are assessed purely by exams. ...., coursework may be employed.

d) ...., there has been growing concern about financing the health service.

e) Many birds use bright colours to attract a mate. ...., flowers advertise their position to fertilising insects.

f) ...., the development should be acceptable environmentally.

cross reference

2.12   *Visual Information*

5. **The following adverbs are used to describe changes in the rate of something:**

Small	Medium	Large
gradually	substantially	quickly
slightly	significantly	sharply
marginally	steadily	dramatically
slowly	considerably	rapidly

Note that certain adverbs are mainly used to describe changes in *time*:
Production in Russia rose *slowly* from 1920 to 1929.

Others are commonly used to show changes in *amount*:
The birth rate increased *slightly* after the revolution.

Label the adverbs in the table above either A (amount) or T (time).

cross reference

2.8   *Numbers*

6. *Use a suitable adverb to complete the following sentences.*

a) Last year inflation increased .... from 2% to 2.3%.

b) Life expectancy has fallen .... in the last 20 years, by about 15%.

c) The price was reduced ...., so that a £12 book was offered for £6.

d) Sales rose .... while he was chairman, averaging 14% per year.

e) The numbers of people voting has declined ...., from 80% to 65%.

f) The crime rate climbed .... in the early1990s, by 20–25% a year.

g) In the last four years unemployment has fallen ...., from 5% to 3.5%.

h) In the first two years of the war the suicide rate dropped ...., by over 30% each year.

3.   Articles

cross reference

3.10   *Nouns: Countable and*
         Uncountable

1. **Unless they are uncountable, all nouns need an article when used in the singular.**

   The article can be either *a/an* or *the*. Compare:

   a)   Research is *an* important activity in universities.

   b)   *The* research begun by Dr Mathews was continued by Professor Brankovic.

   c)   *A* survey was conducted among 200 patients in the clinic.

   In (a) research, which is usually uncountable, is being used in a general sense.

   In (b) a specific piece of research is identified.

   In (c) the survey is not specified and is being mentioned for the first time.

2. **The rules for using *the* (the definite article) are quite complex.**

   Decide why it is used, or not used, in the following examples.

   a)   The most famous fictional detective is Sherlock Holmes.

   b)   The USA was founded in the eighteenth century.

   c)   The government changed its attitude in the 1980s.

   d)   In many companies, the knowledge of most employees is a wasted resource.

   e)   The moon orbits the earth every 28 days.

   f)   The south is characterised by poverty and emigration.

   g)   Charles Dickens, the English novelist, died in 1870.

   h)   The River Trent runs through the middle of England.

   i)   The World Health Organisation was founded in 1948.

3. **In general, *the* is used with:**

   a)   superlatives (*most famous*)

   b)   time periods (*eighteenth century/1980s*)

   c)   unique things (*government/moon/earth*)

   d)   specified things (*knowledge of most employees*)

   e)   regions and rivers (*south/River Trent*)

   f)   very well-known people and things (*English novelist*)

   g)   institutions and bodies (*World Health Organisation*)

   h)   positions (*middle*)

   It is *not* used with:

cross reference

3.8   *Nationality Language*

   i)   names of countries, except for the UK, the USA and a few others

   j)   abstract nouns (*poverty*)

   k)   companies/bodies named after people/places (*Sainsbury's, Sheffield University*)

4. *In the following sentences, decide if the words in italic are specific or not. Insert* **the** *if specific.*

a) .... *engineering* was the main industry in the region.

b) .... *global warming* is partly caused by .... *fossil fuels*.

c) .... *Russian revolution* was partly a result of .... *First World War*.

d) .... *fraud* is costing .... *banking industry* millions of pounds a year.

e) .... *drought* may have been a factor in .... *decline* of the Maya empire.

f) .... *forests of Scandinavia* produce most of .... *world's* paper.

5. *Complete the sentences with either* **the** *or nothing.*

a) .... Japanese emperor lives in .... centre of Tokyo.

b) Already 3% of .... US working population are employed in .... call centres.

c) .... purpose of this paper is to evaluate .... tests of ....intelligence.

d) Picasso, ... Spanish painter, was born in .... nineteenth century.

e) .... best definition is often .... simplest.

6. *Complete the following text by inserting* **a/an/the** *(or nothing) in each gap.*

THE ORIGINS OF @

Giorio Stabile, a) . . . . professor of b) . . . . history at La Sapienza university in Rome, has demonstrated that c) . . . . @ sign, now used in email addresses, was actually invented 500 years ago. Professor Stabile has shown that d) . . . . @, now e) . . . . symbol of f) . . . . internet, was first used by Italian merchants during g) . . . . sixteenth century.

He claims that it originally represented h) . . . . unit of volume, based on i) . . . . large jars used to carry liquids in j) . . . . ancient Mediterranean world. He has found k) . . . . first example of its use in l) . . . . letter written in 1546 by m) . . . . merchant from Florence. n) . . . . letter, which was sent to Rome, announces o) . . . . arrival in p) . . . . Spain of ships carrying gold from South America.

q) . . . . professor argues that r) . . . . @ sign derives from s) . . . . special script used by these merchants, which was developed in t) . . . . sixteenth century. According to him, u) . . . . loop around v) . . . . 'a' is typical of that style. He found w) . . . . evidence while researching x) . . . . visual history of y) . . . . twentieth century.

4.   Caution

cross reference

2.10   *Style*

1. **A cautious style is necessary in some areas of academic writing:**
   Primary products … *usually* have low supply and demand elasticities …
   … multiple factors *may* lead to a psychiatric consultation
   … some parameters *might* depend on the degree of water content in the sand
   … women *tend to* value privacy more than men
   … other studies *suggest* that some permanent modal shift will occur
   Areas where caution is particularly important include:
   a) outlining a hypothesis that needs to be tested, (e.g. in an introduction)
   b) discussing the results of a study, which may not be conclusive
   c) commenting on the work of other writers

cross reference

2.7   *Generalisations*
3.7   *Modal Verbs*

2. **Caution is needed to avoid making statements that are too simplistic:**
   Poor education leads to crime.
   Such statements are rarely completely true. There is usually an exception that needs to be considered. Caution can be shown in several ways:

(modal verb)	Poor education *can* lead to crime.
(adverb)	Poor education *frequently* leads to crime.
(verb/phrase)	Poor education *tends to* lead to crime.
	There is a tendency for poor education to lead to crime.

   Complete the box below with more examples.

Modals	Adverbs	Verb/phrase
can	frequently	tends to
		there is a tendency

3. *Rewrite the following sentences in a more cautious way.*
   a) Private companies are more efficient than state-owned businesses.
   b) Computer manuals are difficult to understand.
   c) Older students perform better at university than younger ones.
   d) Exploring space is a waste of valuable resources.
   e) English pronunciation is confusing.
   f) Global warming will cause the sea level to rise.
   g) Science students work harder than those studying humanities.
   h) Concrete is the best material for building bridges.

cross reference

3.16 Referring Verbs

4. **Another way to express caution is to use *quite, rather* or *fairly* before an adjective.**

a *fairly* accurate summary

quite a significant correlation

a *rather* inconvenient location

NB. *quite* is often used before the article. It is often used positively, whereas *rather* tends to be used negatively.

When referring to sources, the verb used indicates the degree of caution appropriate. Compare:

Widmerpool (1999) *states* that junior doctors work longer than … (positive)

Le Bas (1983) *suggests* that more training would result in …   (cautious)

Other verbs that imply tentative or cautious findings are:

think/consider/hypothesise/believe/claim/presume

5. *Rewrite the following text in more cautious language.*

A team of American scientists have found a way to reverse the ageing process. They fed diet supplements, found in health food shops, to elderly rats, which were then tested for memory and stamina. The animals displayed more active behaviour after taking the supplements, and their memory improved. In addition, their appearance became more youthful and their appetite increased.

The researchers say that this experiment is a clear indication of how the problems of old age can be overcome. They state that in a few years' time everyone will be able to look forward to a long and active retirement.

5.   Conjunctions

1. **Conjunctions are words and phrases such as *and* or *but* which join parts of a sentence together. There are six main types of conjunctions:**

   a) Addition: *Furthermore*, child mortality rates must be examined.

   b) Result: Prices are rising worldwide, *thus* encouraging investment.

   c) Reason: *Owing to* the strike today's classes are cancelled.

   d) Time: *Thirdly*, the role of the architect will be reviewed.

   e) Example: Various writers have examined the issue, *for instance* Van Exel (2000).

   f) Opposition: *Although* this study concentrates mainly on peak-time travellers …

2. *Decide which type (a–f) the following sentences belong to.*

   a) Before the Roman invasion the economy was mainly agricultural.   (…)

   b) The results were checked because they were so surprising.   (…)

   c) Estimates suggest that the effects will continue, but at a more moderate rate.   (…)

   d) Some Asian economies, for example Indonesia, are growing more slowly.   (…)

   e) Moreover, travel information is very important for route planning.   (…)

   f) The findings were ambiguous, therefore the study was revised.   (…)

   g) The deadline is next week, so speed is vital.   (…)

   h) There is a serious problem in the district; namely unemployment.   (…)

3. *Complete the table to show as many examples of conjunctions as possible.*

Addition	Result	Reason	Time	Example	Opposition
furthermore	thus	owing to	thirdly	for instance	although

4. *Insert a suitable conjunction in each gap.*

   a) …………… the course was voluntary only seven students attended.
   b) The longest day of the year, …………… June 21st, was a time of festivity.
   c) …………… the equipment was checked the experiment was repeated.
   d) …………… most people use the train, a minority walk or cycle.
   e) Brick is a thermally efficient building material. It is, ……………, cheap.
   f) Demand has increased for summer courses, …………… extra ones are offered this year.

5. *Complete the following biography by inserting suitable conjunctions.*

   THE BEATLES

   The group which became the Beatles was formed in 1960 by John Lennon and Paul McCartney, with George Harrison and Ringo Starr joining later. a) ………… playing in small clubs for two years their first record, *Love Me Do,* was released. *She Loves You*, in 1963, broke all previous sales records in Britain. b) ………… their simplicity, the early Beatles songs c) ………… *Yesterday* and *Paperback Writer* are still seen as masterpieces of musical genius. d) …………, the unusual haircuts and clothes worn by the Beatles fitted well with the style of the mid-1960s. The popularity of the group soon spread to the USA and e) ………… around the world, f) ………… the media invented the term 'Beatlemania' to describe the excitement that was part of their tours. g) ………… their popularity the group were awarded the MBE by the Queen in 1965, h) ………… this caused anger among some of the older holders of this award.

   In 1966 the Beatles stopped live performances, i) ………… their music was becoming too complex to produce on stage. A year later *Sgt. Pepper's Lonely Hearts Club Band* was released, j) …………was immediately recognised as one of the most influential works in the history of popular music. k) …………, the pressures of fame were beginning to affect all the members of the band, l) ………… that they found it harder to work together. They played together for the last time in 1969 and m) ………… split up in 1970.

6. **Conjunctions of opposition**

   Note the position of the conjunctions in the following examples.
   The economy is strong, *but/yet* there are frequent strikes.
   Although there are frequent strikes, the economy is strong.
   In spite of/despite the frequent strikes, the economy is strong.
   There are frequent strikes. *However/nevertheless*, the economy is strong.

Write two sentences in each case.

Example: The equipment was expensive/unreliable.

The equipment was expensive but unreliable.

Although the equipment was expensive, it was unreliable.

a)   The government claimed that inflation was falling. The opposition said it was rising.

   i)

   ii)

b)   This department must reduce expenditure. It needs to install new computers.

   i)

   ii)

7. *Finish the sentences in a suitable way.*

   a)   In contrast to America, where gun ownership is common, ...

   b)   Despite leaving school at the age of 14, ...

   c)   The majority displayed a positive attitude to the proposal, but ....

   d)   The review has examined six studies of medical policy; however ....

   e)   Although the spring was cold and dry, ...

6.   Formality in Verbs

2.10   *Style*

1. A feature of most academic writing is a tendency to use rather formal verbs to express the writer's meaning accurately:

… supply of energy required to *accelerate* the growth …

… the development that is *envisaged* here needs to be not only sustainable …

In spoken English we would be more likely to use *speed up* and *imagined*.

cross reference

2.11   *Synonyms*
3.14   *Prepositions after Verbs*

2. *Study the list below and find the meaning in each case.*

NB. Some of these verbs, e.g. *hold*, are used in academic writing with a special meaning.

Verb	Example of use
to adapt	the health system has been *adapted* from France
to arise	a similar situation *arises* when we look at younger children
to carry out	the largest study was *carried out* in Finland
to characterise	developing countries are *characterised* by ….
to clarify	the project was designed to *clarify* these contradictions
to concentrate on	that study *concentrated on* older children
to be concerned with	the programme is *concerned* primarily *with* …
to demonstrate	further research has *demonstrated* that few factors …
to determine	the water content was experimentally *determined*
to discriminate	a failure to *discriminate* between the two species
to emphasise	the 1987 report *emphasised* energy efficiency
to establish	the northern boundary was *established* first
to exhibit	half of the patients *exhibited* signs of improvement
to focus on	her work *focused on* female managers
to generate	a question that has *generated* a range of responses
to hold	Newton's second law, $F = ma$, *holds* everywhere …
to identify	three main areas have been *identified*
to imply	previous research *implies* that size is a good predictor
to indicate	all the surveys *indicate* that employees prefer pay rises
to interact	understand how the two systems *interact*
to interpret	the conclusion can be *interpreted* as a limited success
to manifest	as *manifested* in anti-social behaviour
to overcome	both difficulties were *overcome* in the first week
to predict	the study *predicts* that productivity will decline next year
to propose	they *propose* that social class is the main factor

to prove	the use of solar power is *proving* successful
to recognise	he is now *recognised* as a leading expert
to relate to	the pattern was *related to* both social and physical factors
to supplement	the diet was *supplemented* with calcium and iodine
to undergo	the system *underwent* major changes in the 1980s
to yield	both surveys *yielded* mixed results

3. *Select the better alternative in each case.*

   a) The survey *proved/yielded* a surprising amount of information on student politics.

   b) This question *arose/manifested* when older students were examined.

   c) Both writers attempt to *demonstrate/imply* that older employees are more reliable.

   d) Darwin *held/indicated* very strong views on this issue.

   e) It must be *proved/emphasised* that these results are only provisional.

   f) One of the chimpanzees *supplemented/exhibited* signs of nervousness.

   g) Freud was *concerned/identified* primarily with middle-class patients.

   h) The study was *generated/carried out* to explore the issue of religious tolerance.

4. *Insert a suitable verb from the box below into each gap.*

| overcome | predict | demonstrate | interpret |
| discriminate | recognise | clarify | focus on |

   a) The results clearly .... that younger children learn more quickly.

   b) This paper attempts to .... the confusion surrounding studies of infertility.

   c) Social class must be .... as a leading factor in educational success.

   d) His study fails to .... between the various types of reinforced concrete.

   e) Most experts failed to .... the collapse of Soviet power in 1989.

   f) It seems profitable to .... the record of smaller companies.

   g) The noises made by whales have been .... in several ways.

   h) This problem was .... by reversing the direction of the gas flow.

7.   Modal Verbs

1. **Modal verbs used in academic writing tend to have three main meanings:**

   a) **Ability**

   May and *can* are similar but *can* is more common:

   The assessment ... *may* be made in a variety of ways

   ... with smaller samples this method *cannot* be used ...

   ... one faculty *can* have more than one academic programme ...

cross reference

3.4   *Caution*

   b) **Degrees of certainty**

   Will and *should* are used for predictions of near certainty (*will* is stronger):

   ... in the knowledge that the parent *will* be there when needed

   Improved facilities *should* lead to lower staff turnover

   May and *might* both suggest possibility:

   Landfill carbon sequestration *might* supplement fossil fuel combustion ...

   ... multiple factors *may* lead to a psychiatric consultation ...

   Would and *could* are used in conditional situations (not always with *if*):

   ... or *would* we conclude that the observation is uninformative?

   ... estimates of the model's parameters *could* conceivably be computed ...

   c) **Degrees of obligation**

   Must suggests strong obligation; *should* is for recommendations:

   To obtain a total estimate ... several approximations *must* be used

   A primary research emphasis ... *should* then be on identifying ...

2. *Complete the following sentences with a suitable modal of ability.*

   a) The question is whether democracy .... survive in such difficult conditions.

   b) Fifty years ago a new house .... be bought for £1500.

   c) Students .... be expected to write more than one long essay a week.

   d) The mistakes of past historians .... now be clearly seen.

   e) Jenkins (1976) argued that aluminium .... be used in place of steel.

3. *Complete the following with a suitable modal of certainty.*

   a) It .... not be surprising if the company were bought by a rival.

   b) Various social situations .... lead to a child's loss of confidence.

   c) Other studies confirm that a permanent shift in transport use .... occur.

   d) By 2020 most children .... have internet access by the age of five.

   e) If the pressure is lowered, the reaction .... take place more quickly.

f) In the long term, solar power .... make a significant
    contribution.

4. *Use a suitable modal of obligation to complete the following.*

    a) Students studying abroad.............. take some of their favourite music
        with them.
    b) All books.............. be returned to the main library by June 19th.
    c) First-year undergraduates.............. take at least three modules from
        the list below.
    d) The second part of the essay.............. focus on the differences in the
        results.

5. *In the following sentences, the meaning changes according to the modal verb
    used. Find two possibilities, giving the meanings in each case.*

    Example:

    Using the internet means the company *can* sell its products worldwide. (ability)

    Using the internet means the company *might* sell its products worldwide. (possibility)

    a) The poorest people.............. be helped by improving the
        supply of water   (......)
        The poorest people.............. be helped by improving the
        supply of water   (......)
    b) Tribal leaders of the 1st century BC.............. have used writing.   (......)
        Tribal leaders of the 1st century BC .... have used writing. (......)
    c) Few people.............. agree to take part in the experiment.   (......)
        Few people.............. agree to take part in the experiment.   (......)
    d) Care.............. always be taken when interpreting 19th-century
        data.   (......)
        Care.............. always be taken when interpreting 19th-century
        data.   (......)
    e) By the mid-21st century poverty.............. be abolished.   (......)
        By the mid-21st century poverty.............. be abolished.   (......)
    f) Repeating the study.............. confirm their findings.   (......)
        Repeating the study.. .... confirm their findings.   (......)

8.   Nationality Language

1. Most nationalities have a regular pattern of nouns and adjectives.

Germany is a leading industrial economy.	(country)
The *German* capital is Berlin.	(adjective)
German is spoken by over 100 million.	(language)
Germans/The Germans like wine.	(people)

Most national adjectives end in *-an/-ian/-ish/-ch/-ese/-i.*

2. Some nationalities are less regular.

Holland/The Netherlands is located between Belgium and Germany.

The *Dutch* capital is The Hague.

Dutch is related to German.

Dutch people often speak English well.

Country	People	Country	People	Country	People
Denmark	Danes	Iraq	Iraqis	Switzerland	Swiss
Greece	Greeks	Pakistan	Pakistanis	Chile	Chileans
Poland	Poles	Thailand	Thais	Portugal	Portuguese

3. *Write similar sentences to those above about* **two** *of the following:*

France	Japan	Egypt	India	Ireland	Mexico

i)   i)

ii)   ii)

iii)   iii)

iv)   iv)

cross reference

3.3 *Articles*

4. The definite article is used with a few countries:

The United Arab Emirates

The United States

The United Kingdom

The Czech Republic

With national adjectives ending in *–an/-ian* it is possible to say, for example:

Italians/The Italians/Italian people have enjoyed opera for over 200 years.

With other endings the first form is not possible:

The Japanese/Japanese people like watching sumo wrestling.

NB. *England* is not a political unit. Although it is possible to use *English people/English food*, the nationality is *British*. The country's name is *Britain* or the *United Kingdom*.

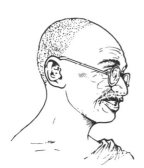

5. *Complete the spaces in the following sentences with* **one** *word.*
   a) Beijing is the .... capital.
   b) The rouble is the .... currency.
   c) The largest city in .... is Sydney.
   d) Many .... people enjoy going to bullfights.
   e) Nelson Mandela was the .... president.
   f) .... are the only South Americans who speak Portuguese.
   g) The .... capital is Baghdad.
   h) .... speak Spanish and make fine cigars.

6. *Write sentences about some of the people in the box, giving their nationality.*

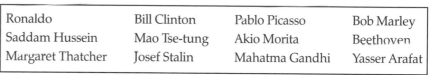

Ronaldo	Bill Clinton	Pablo Picasso	Bob Marley
Saddam Hussein	Mao Tse-tung	Akio Morita	Beethoven
Margaret Thatcher	Josef Stalin	Mahatma Gandhi	Yasser Arafat

Example:
Ronaldo is a Brazilian footballer/Ronaldo comes from Brazil.
a)
b)
c)
d)
e)
f)
g)
h)

9.   Nouns and Adjectives

1. *Compare these sentences:*

The *efficiency* of the machine depends on the *precision* of its construction.

Precise construction results in an *efficient* machine.

The first sentence uses the nouns *efficiency* and *precision*. The second uses adjectives: *precise* and *efficient*. Although the meaning is similar the first sentence is more formal. Effective academic writing requires accurate use of both forms, which can be easily confused.

2. *Underline and correct the mistakes in the following:*

a)   Some areas of the capital are not safety.

b)   Various culture patterns in French society need to be considered.

c)   The deep of the lake is calculated at 550 metres.

d)   A health diet includes fresh fruit and vegetables.

3. *Complete the gaps in the table below.*

Noun	Adjective	Noun	Adjective	Noun	Adjective
height		reliability		heat	
	strong		confident		true
width		probability		necessity	
	long		dangerous		relevant

4. *Insert a suitable noun or adjective from the table in each sentence.*

a)   These data appear not to be .... and should not be trusted.

b)   The .... of the matter may never be known, since all the records are lost.

c)   There is a strong .... that coffee prices will fall next year.

d)   In some places the River Zambesi is more than three kilometres ....

e)   The results are so surprising it will be .... to repeat the experiment.

f)   It is not easy to see the .... of art history to engineering.

g)   Regularly backing-up computer files reduces the .... of losing vital work.

h)   Revising for exams is a tedious ....

i)   The building's .... is due to its massive steel frame.

j)   .... in the banking system was destroyed by years of inflation.

5. *Underline the adjective(s) in each sentence for which it is possible to form a related noun. Write the noun in brackets.*

Example:

Few patients are <u>likely</u> to suffer side-effects from the drug. (likelihood)

a) Various methods of dealing with the spread of malaria were
   suggested.   (.........)
b) Dr Lee adopted an analytical approach to the inquiry.   (.........)
c) Antibiotics were not available in the first half of the
   20th century.   (.........)
d) Her major contribution to the research was her study of
   folklore in Spain.   (.........)
e) The precise number of people affected by the earthquake
   is unknown.   (.........) (.........)
f) Some progress was made in the theoretical area.   (.........)
g) A frequent complaint is that too much work is expected
   in the first semester.   (.........)
h) We took a more critical approach to irrigation.   (.........)
i) The Department of Social Policy is offering three
   courses this year.   (.........)
j) Finally, the practical implications of my findings will be
   examined.   (.........)

6. *Complete the gaps in the table below.*

Noun	Adjective	Noun	Adjective
approximation	approximate		particular
superiority		reason	
	strategic		synthetic
politics		economy	
	industrial		cultural
exterior		average	

7. *Complete the sentences with nouns or adjectives from the table above.*
   a) The...................consequences of the war were inflation and
      unemployment.
   b) 365.25 days is an...................of the length of the solar year.
   c) One...................of British weather is that it is very changeable.
   d) All...................doors are fitted with security systems.
   e) They attempted to make a...................of all the different proposals.
   f) The...................length of time patients have to wait is 34.6 weeks.
   g) The traditional idea that the sun went round the earth
      was..................., but wrong.
   h) Ancient Japanese...................was highly developed in areas such as
      poetry and ceramics.

10. Nouns: Countable and Uncountable

1. **Most nouns in English are countable, but the following are generally uncountable, i.e. they are not usually used with numbers or the plural 's'.**

accommodation	information	scenery
advice	knowledge	staff
behaviour	money	traffic
commerce	news	travel
data	permission	trouble
education	progress	vocabulary
equipment	research	weather
furniture	rubbish	work

cross reference

3.18 Singular/Plural

2. **Another group of uncountable nouns is used for materials:**

wood/rubber/iron/coffee/paper/water/oil/stone

Little *wood* is used in the construction of motor vehicles.

Huge amounts of *paper* are used to produce magazines.

Many of these nouns can be used as countable nouns with a rather different meaning:

Over twenty daily *papers* are published in Delhi.

Many *woods* in the county have a long recorded history.

3. **The most difficult group can be used either as countable or uncountable nouns, often with quite different meanings.**

She developed *an interest* in bio-genetics.

The bank is paying 4% *interest* on six-month deposits.

Other nouns with a similar pattern are used for general concepts (*love/fear/hope*).

Most people feel that *life* is too short. (in general)

Nearly twenty *lives* were lost in the mining accident. (in particular)

Complete the following sentences to show the differences in meaning.

a) Three years' experience...

b) She had some exciting experiences while...............................

c) Most small businesses have...

d) In many countries it is normal to discuss business...............

e) A number of capitals such as Washington and Canberra are................

f) Huge amounts of capital...

g) Two world wars in thirty years caused....................................

h) War is a feature of..

i) ....was the cause of six deaths.

j) Death is..

k) New medicines are developed..

l) Studying medicine at university can be....................................

4. *Note the importance of the type of noun in the following structures:*

Questions: *How much accommodation* (U) is available for rent?

                        How many rooms (C) are vacant next month?

Negatives: *Not much/Little equipment* (U) was needed for the experiment.

                        Not many/Few machines (C) were functioning in the IT room.

5. *In the following sentences, choose the correct alternative.*

a)   *Little/few* news reached the prisoners in the castle.

b)   He established three successful *businesses/business* in 1995.

c)   Substantial *experiences/experience* of report writing *are/is* required.

d)   It has often been claimed that *travel broadens/travels broaden* the mind.

e)   *Paper was/papers were* very expensive in the Middle Ages.

f)   How *much advice/many advices* were they given before coming to Britain?

g)   She had *little interest/few interests* outside her work.

h)   The insurance policy excludes the effects of civil *war/wars*.

i)   *Irons were/iron was* first powered by electricity in the twentieth century.

j)   They studied the *behaviour/behaviours* of three groups of lions over two years.

6. *Complete the gaps in the following paragraph with* **much/many/little/few.**

Very a) . . . . data is available to students of housing of the 6th–9th centuries A.D. No

complete examples survive, and researchers are not certain how b) . . . . .information can

be taken from the literature. It is not clear how c) . . . . .people lived in each house, and in

the d) . . . . sites that have been investigated (only four in the whole country)

e) . . . . progress has been made towards finding a standard floor plan.

11. Passives

2.10   *Style*

1. The passive is used when the writer wants to focus on the result, not on the cause:

The book was written *in 1926*. (passive)

My father wrote the book. (active)

In the first sentence, the emphasis is on the date, in the second on the writer. So the passive is used in written English when the cause (a person or thing) is less important or unknown.

The treaty *will be signed* next year. (by someone)

The tower *was destroyed* a century ago. (by something)

It is quite common to show the cause of the action by adding *by …*

The army was helped *by good weather* in the autumn of 1296.

2. The passive is also used in written work to avoid using *I* or *we*:

The findings *were evaluated*.

An analysis *will be made*.

Change the following into the passive.

a)   We collected the data and compared the two groups.

b)   I interviewed 120 people in three social classes.

c)   They checked the results and found several errors.

cross reference

3.2   *Adverbs*

3. An adverb is often inserted in a passive form:

This process *is commonly called* 'networking'.

Change the following sentences from active to passive and insert a suitable adverb from the box below.

a)   A storm damaged 40% of the houses in the port.

b)   The Connors family ran the company until 1981.

c)   They had built the house near the station.

d)   Picasso painted the portrait of the old man.

e)   They provided pencils for all students in the exam.

f)   Doctors tested over 550 people for the disease over a three-year period.

g)   The researchers calculated the percentages to three decimal places.

h)   They called their business the Universal Trading Company.

| conveniently | optimistically | helpfully | brilliantly |
| regularly | precisely | efficiently | badly |

4. In most texts the active and the passive are mixed.
Read the following article and underline the passives.

BOOTS THE CHEMISTS

When John Boot died at 45, he was worn out by the strain of establishing his herbal medicine business. He had worked his way up from his early years as a farm labourer to be the owner of a substantial business. He was born in 1815, became a member of a Methodist chapel in Nottingham, and later moved to the city. Concerned by the situation of the poor, who were unable to afford a doctor, in 1849 he opened a herbal medicine shop which was called the British and American Botanic Establishment. In the early stages John was helped financially by his father-in-law, while his mother provided herbal knowledge.

On his death in 1860 the business was taken over by his wife, and she was soon assisted by their 10-year-old son, Jesse. He quickly showed the business ability which transformed his father's shop into a national business. He opened more shops in poor districts of the city and pioneered advertising methods. Another innovation was to do all his business in cash, rather than offering credit.

5. *Could all the passives in the text be replaced by the active? What would be the result if most of them were?*

6. The passive is used more in written than in spoken English, but should not be over-used, because it can give a very formal tone.
In the following text, which continues the history of Boots, the passive is used throughout. Change some of them into the active.

In 1889 he was introduced to Florence Rowe, the daughter of a bookseller, while on holiday. Her influence was felt by the business after they were married: the product range was enlarged to include stationery and books. In addition she was responsible for the introduction of the Boots subscription library and in-store cafes.

During World War 1 the factories were used to make a variety of products from sterilizers to gas masks. But by 1920 Jesse was being attacked by arthritis and was worried by the economic prospects. Boots was sold to an American rival for £2 m. This, however, was made bankrupt during the Depression and Boots was then bought by a British group for £6 m, while Jesse's son, John, was made chairman. The famous No. 7 cosmetics range was launched in the 1930s. In the 1939–45 War the saccharin equivalent to 700,000 tons of sugar was produced in the Nottingham factories.

12. Prefixes and Suffixes

1. *Automatically* and *uncontrollable* are examples of words containing prefixes and suffixes. Words like these are much easier to understand if you know how prefixes and suffixes affect word meaning.

   Prefixes change or give the meaning.

   Suffixes show the meaning or the word class.

Prefix	Meaning	Suffix	Word class/meaning
auto-	by itself	-ally	adverb
un-	negative	-able	ability

   The machine started *automatically*.

   The class of young boys was *uncontrollable*.

2. **Prefixes.**

   a) Negative prefixes. *un-*, *in-*, *mis-* and *dis-* often give adjectives and verbs a negative meaning: *un*clear, *in*sane, *mis*hear, *dis*agree.

   b) A wide variety of prefixes define meaning, e.g. *pre-* usually means *before*; hence *pre*fer, *pre*history and, of course, *pre*fix.

3. **Common prefixes.**

   Find the meaning(s) of each prefix.

   NB. Some prefixes have more than one meaning.

auto	autopilot	The plane flew on *autopilot* for six hours
co	co-ordinator	The *co-ordinator* invited them to a meeting
ex	ex-girlfriend	He met his *ex-girlfriend* on the station
ex	exclusive	It is difficult to join such an *exclusive* club
micro	microscope	She studied the tiny animals with a *microscope*
multi	multinational	Ford is a *multi-national* motor company
over	oversleep	After *oversleeping* twice she got an alarm clock
post	postpone	The meeting is *postponed* to next Monday
re	return	*Return* the letter to the sender
sub	subtitle	Chinese films have *subtitles* in England
under	undergraduate	Most *undergraduate* courses last 3 years
under	undercook	*Undercooked* meat can be a health hazard

   N.B. Some prefixes have more than one meaning

4. *Suggest possible meanings for the words in italic.*

   a) Criminal activity seems to be very common among the *underclass*.

   b) The passengers found the jet was *overbooked* and had to wait for the next flight.

   c) The *microclimate* in my garden means that I can grow oranges.

   d) It is claimed that computers have created a *post-industrial* economy.

   e) Most film stars have *ex-directory* phone numbers.

   f) It is believed that dreams are produced by the *subconscious*.

5. **Suffixes.**

   a) Some suffixes like *-ion, -ive* or *-ly* help the reader find the word class.

   b) Other suffixes add to meaning, e.g. *-ful* or *-less* after an adjective have a positive or negative effect (thought*ful*/thought*less*).

6. **Word class suffixes.**

nouns	-er often indicates a person: *teacher, gardener*
	-ee shows the person who is the subject: *trainer/trainee*
	-ism and -ist are used with belief systems and their supporters: *capitalism/capitalist*
	-ness converts an adjective into a noun: *sad/sadness*
	-ion changes a verb to a noun: *convert/conversion*
adjectives	-ive: *effective, constructive*
	-al: *commercial, agricultural*
	-ous: *precious, serious*
verbs	-ise/-ize to form verbs from adjectives: *private/privatise*
adverbs	-ly; most (but not all) adverbs have this suffix: *happily*

7. **Meaning suffixes.**

A few suffixes contribute to the meaning of the word:

-able has the meaning of *ability*: a *watchable* film, *changeable* weather

-wards means *in the direction of*: the ship sailed *northwards*

-ful and *-less*: *hopeful* news, a *leaderless* army

8. *Give the word class and suggest possible meanings for:*

   a) cancellation

   b) unpredictable

   c) coincidental

   d) saleable

   e) uncooperatively

   f) interviewee

   g) evolutionary

   h) surrealism

   i) protester

   j) symbolically

9. *Study each sentence and find the meaning of the words in italic.*
   a) The film is a French–Italian *co-production* made by a *subsidiary* company.
   b) When the car crashed she screamed *involuntarily* but was *unharmed*.
   c) Using *rechargeable* batteries has *undoubted* benefits for the environment.
   d) The *unavailability* of the product is due to the *exceptional* weather.
   e) There is a *theoretical* possibility of the cloth *disintegrating*.

13. Prepositions

cross reference

3.14 Prepositions after Verbs

1. *Underline the prepositions in the following text.*

The purpose of this paper is to examine the development of the textile industry in Britain over the period 1750–1850. This clearly contributed to the nation's industrialisation, and was valuable for stimulating exports. In conclusion, the paper sets out to demonstrate the relationship between the decline in agricultural employment and the supply of cheap labour in the factory context.

The table lists the main ways of using prepositions.
Find one example of each in the text.

noun + preposition	purpose of
verb + preposition	
adjective + preposition	
phrasal verb	
preposition of place	
preposition of time	
phrase	

NB. The difference between phrasal verbs and verbs with prepositions:
The cars are *made in* Korea. (verb + preposition = easy to understand)
The writer *made up* the story in a night. (phrasal verb – hard to understand)

2. *Study these further examples of preposition use and decide on their type.*

a) There are a number *of* limitations to be considered …   (noun +)
b) The results would be applicable *to* all managers …   (……)
c) … the data was gathered *from* a questionnaire   (……)
d) All the items were placed *within* their categories   (……)
e) The results *of* the investigation are still pertinent …   (……)
f) The respondents had spent *on* average 4.9 years …   (……)
g) … most countries *in* sub-Saharan Africa …   (……)
h) … *within* a short spell of four years   (……)

3. *Insert a suitable preposition before or after the nouns in the sentences below.*

a) Evidence is presented in support…..the value of women's work.
b) A small change…..demand can lead to large price rises.
c) Many examples were found…..high levels of calcium.
d) We tried to assess the feasibility…..allowing children to choose their own subjects.
e) The second point is their impact…..developing countries.

4. *Complete the following phrases with the correct prepositions.*

a) …..the whole
b) point ….. view

c)   in respect .....

d)   ..... spite of

e)   in support .....

5.   *Complete the following sentences with suitable prepositions of place or time.*

   a)   ....the respondents, few had any experience of working abroad.

   b)   Industrial production declined gradually .... 1976 .... 1985.

   c)   Most workers .... the European Union retire before the age ....60.

   d)   Albert Einstein was born .... Germany .... 1879.

   e)   Many flowers open their petals .... the morning and close them .... night.

   f)   .... the surface, there is no difference .... male and female responses.

6.   *Complete the text with suitable prepositions.*

This study sets a) .... to answer the controversial question b) .... whether increased food supply c) .... a country makes a significant contribution d) .... reducing malnutrition e) .... children. It uses data collected f) .... 75 countries g) .... 1969 and 1987. The findings are that there was a considerable improvement h) .... the majority i) .... countries, despite population increases j) .... the period. However, a clear distinction was found k) .... the poorest countries (e.g. l) .... South Asia), where the improvement was greatest, and the wealthier states such as those m) .... North Africa. Other factors, notably the educational level n) .... women, were also found to be critical o) .... improving childhood nutrition.

14. Prepositions after Verbs

cross reference

3.6   *Formality in Verbs*
3.13   *Prepositions*

1. The following verbs are generally used with these prepositions:

Verb + prep.	Example
add to	The bad weather *added to* the General's difficulties.
agree with	Yu (1977) *agrees with* Martin and Jenks (1989).
associate with	Monetarism is an economic policy *associated with* Mrs Thatcher.
believe in	The survey showed that 65% *believed in* life after death.
blame for	He *blamed* unfair questions *for* his poor exam results.
concentrate on*	She dropped all her hobbies to *concentrate on* her work.
consist of	Parliament *consists of* two Houses: the Commons and the Lords.
depend on*	The company *depends on* IT for a rapid flow of sales data.
derive from	All modern computers *derive from* wartime decoding machines.
divide into	Trees are *divided into* two main types: conifers and deciduous.
invest in	Far more money needs to be *invested in* primary education.
learn from	All successful students *learn from* their mistakes.
pay for	Goods delivered in April must be *paid for* by June 30th.
point out	Goodson (2001) *points out* the dangers of over-specialisation.
specialise in	This department *specialises in* French-Canadian poetry.

* *focus* on and *rely on* are similar.

2. *Complete the following with suitable verbs and prepositions.*

a) The enquiry................the cause of the accident, not the consequences.

b) Dr Cracknell..................that there were only two weeks before the deadline.

c) Fewer British students are..................foreign languages.

d) The theory of relativity will always be..................Albert Einstein.

e) A football pitch is..................two halves.

f) A series of strikes were..................the decline in production during May.

g) Millions of men died for the cause they..................

h) Every nation needs a public transport system it can..................

3. With the following verbs more than one preposition is possible. Note the change of meaning in some cases.

Verb + preposition	Example
compare to/with	The stock market has been *compared with/to* a casino.
look at/into	The evidence needs to be *looked at/into* more carefully.
look for	Most students use search engines to *look for* information.
apply to	He *applied to* the committee for a grant.
apply for	To *apply for* the job three forms must be completed.

4. *Choose suitable verbs and prepositions from (1) and (3) to complete the following text.*

The new model of camera, the Alpha 616, a) .... the previous model, the 615. The Alpha 616 b) .... a standard camera with a small tape recorder c) .... it. This allows the photographer to talk to the camera. The marketing unit d) .... the camera market carefully and discovered that many people forget where they take pictures. These people can now e) .... the Alpha 616 to remember for them.

The company has f) .... over £2 million .... the new product. g) .... other projects this may seem a small amount, but this is not a large business. It is hoped that customers will h). .... over £100 .... the camera, which the company will i) .... for significant profits next year.

15. Punctuation

1. **Capitals.**

   It is difficult to give precise rules about the use of capital letters in modern English. However, they should be used in the following cases:

   a) The first word in a sentence   *In the beginning…*
   b) Names of organisations   *Sheffield Hallam University*
   c) Days and months   *Friday 21st July*
   d) Nationality words   *France and the French*
   e) Names of people/places   *Dr Martin Turner from Edinburgh*
   f) Titles (capitalise main words only) *The Uses of Literacy/The Duke of Kent*

2. **Apostrophes (').**

   These are one of the most misused features of English punctuation. They are mainly used in two situations:

   a) to show contractions   *It's generally believed …*

   NB. Contractions are not common in academic English.

   b) with possessives   *The professor's secretary* (singular)

                                          Students' marks (plural)

3. **Semi-colons (;).**

   These are used to show the link between two connected phrases when a comma would be too weak and a full stop too strong.

   Twenty people were interviewed for the first study; thirty-three for the second.

   Semi-colons are also used to divide up items in a list when they have a complex structure:

   Among the presents received by the president were three oil paintings of himself, all flattering; a pair of green parrots, which were very noisy; a solid gold medal and three or four suits of clothes.

   NB. Semi-colons are quite rare in most types of writing.

4. **Colons (:).**

   a) to introduce explanations   *The meeting was postponed: the Dean was ill.*

   b) to start a list   *Two factors were discussed: cultural and social.*

   c) to introduce a quotation   *As Orwell said: 'all art is propaganda'.*

| cross reference |
| 2.9 *References and Quotations* |

5. **Quotation marks/inverted commas ('…' / "…").**

   a) single quotation marks are used to emphasise a word, to give quotations from other writers and to show direct speech:

   The word 'quiz' was first used in the nineteenth century.
   Goodwin's (1977) analysis of habit … indicates that, in general, 'it will be more difficult to reverse a trend than to accentuate it'.

   'Can anyone find the answer?' asked the lecturer.

NB. Longer quotations are usually indented (i.e. have a wider margin) or are set in smaller type.

b) double quotation marks are used to show quotations inside quotations (nested quotations):

As Murphy has observed: 'Concepts of "typical" need careful examination.'

c) quotation marks are used for the names of articles and chapters, but book and journal titles use italics.

6. **Other punctuation marks.**

Hyphens (-) are used with certain words and structures:

well-engineered/co-operative/three-year-old

Exclamation marks (!) and question marks (?):

'Well!' he shouted. 'Who would believe it?'

Brackets (…) are used to contain information of lesser importance:

There were only 31 marriages (out of 13,829) in which 'baker' was listed.

7. *Punctuate the following sentences.*

a) on tuesday june 6 1759 in the church at derby nicolas james married mary dewey

b) professor rowans new book the triumph of capitalism is published in new york

c) how many people would agree with john lennon when he said all you need is love

d) the probability was calculated for each of the three faculties physics biology and law

e) as cammack 1994 points out latin america is creating a new phenomenon democracy without citizens

f) thousands of new words such as website enter the english language each year

g) dr tanners latest study focuses on childrens reactions to stress in the playground

h) she scored 56% on the main course the previous semester she had achieved 67%

8. *Punctuate the text.*

the london school of business is offering three new courses this year economics with psychology introduction to management and ecommerce the first is taught by dr jennifer hillary and runs from october to january the second introduction to management for msc finance students is offered in the second semester and is assessed by coursework only professor wangs course in ecommerce runs in both the autumn and the spring and is for more experienced students

16. Referring Verbs

1. **Referring verbs are used to summarise another writer's ideas.**

   Wilsher *argued* that the single play had been consigned to television history.

   Heffernan (1972) *found* that adaptation to prison was facilitated by …

   They may also be used to introduce a quotation from the writer.

   … as Peter Huber has *observed*, 'Coal itself is yesterday's landfill …'

2. **Most of these verbs are followed by a noun clause beginning with** *that*.

   a) The following mean that the writer is presenting a case:

       argue   claim   consider   hypothesise   suggest   believe   think   state

   Martins (1975) *claimed* that many mergers led to lower profits.

   b) A second group describes a reaction to another writer's position:

       accept   admit   agree   deny   doubt

   Handlesmith *doubts* Martins's claim that lower profits resulted from …

   c) Others include:

       assume   conclude   discover   explain   imply   indicate   maintain   presume
       reveal   show

3. *Write a sentence referring to what the following writers said (more than one verb may be suitable).*

   Example:

   Z: 'My research shows that cats are cleverer than dogs.'

   Z claimed/argued that cats were cleverer than dogs.

   a) A: 'You could be right. I may have made a mistake in my estimate.'

   b) B: 'I did not say that sheep were faster than horses.'

   c) C: 'Whales are very intelligent animals.'

   d) D: 'I support A's position on cats and dogs.'

   e) E: 'I'm not sure, but cows probably get cold in winter.'

f)   F: 'After much research, I've found that pigs can't fly.'

g)   G: 'On my travels in the jungle I found a new type of frog.'

h)   H: 'I think it unlikely that cats can learn to talk.'

i)   I: 'Somebody should compare mouse behaviour with rat behaviour.'

j)   J: 'There may be a link between health and the seasons.'

4. **A small group of verbs is followed by (somebody/something + *for* + noun/gerund):**
    Lee (1998) *blamed* foreign investors for the panic.
    blame   censure   commend   condemn   criticise
    NB. All except *commend* have a negative meaning.
    A final group is followed by (somebody/something + *as* + noun/gerund):
    Terry *interprets* rising oil prices as a response to Asian recovery.
    assess   characterise   classify   define   describe   evaluate   identify
    interpret   portray   present

5. *Re-write the following statements using verbs from the lists in (4).*
    a)   K: 'X's work is responsible for a lot of our current economic problems.'

    b)   L: 'She was very careless about her research methods.'

    c)   M: 'There are three main species of bees.'

    d)   N: 'The cat family are the kings of the animal world.'

    e)   O: 'I'm sure that dogs bark because they are nervous.'

    f)   P: 'Trying to estimate the number of animal species is like shooting in the dark.'

    g)   Q: 'Darwin was the greatest naturalist of the nineteenth century.'

    h)   R: 'An insect is a six-legged arthropod.'

    i)   S: 'Queen Victoria was a short, rather fat woman with dark eyes.'

    j)   T: 'Gregor Mendel can be considered the founder of modern genetics.'

17. Relative Pronouns

1. **Relative pronouns (*who/whose/where/which/that*) introduce a relative clause.**

   The journal, *which* was edited by my tutor, was missing from the library.

   The college *where* he studied has been given £4 million.

   The teacher *who* interviewed me was a specialist in ancient music.

   Dr Yamada, *whose* lecture I attended, presented the prizes.

   He wrote about the area *that* I was interested in.

   Which relative pronouns are used for:

   a) places?

   b) people?

   c) things?

   d) possession?

2.4   *Definitions*

2. *Insert a suitable relative pronoun in these sentences.*

   a) The book................he wanted had been borrowed by someone else.

   b) Beijing,................she studied for six months, used to be called Peking.

   c) Charlie Chaplin,................was born in England, was a great film comedian.

   d) A hydrometer is an instrument................is used to measure density in liquids.

   e) Few people have heard of the man................invented television.

   f) Mercury,................is a liquid element, is used in many industrial processes.

3. **As can be seen from the examples above, there are two kinds of relative clauses:**

   a) Those which define the subject. In this case the relative clause must be included:

   The college *where he studied* has been given £4 million.

   b) Those which give additional details:

   The journal, *which was edited by my tutor*, was missing from the library.

   Here the relative clause could be removed and the meaning would still be clear.

   In this second type the relative clause is surrounded by commas (,), brackets or dashes (–)

4. *Decide if the following sentences contain defining (D) or additional detail (A) clauses.*

   a) Akio Morita was the person who invented the Walkman.

   b) The first thing that he did was to introduce a new system of assessment.

   c) The medical school, which has a very good reputation, charges £20,000 per year.

d)   The president (who enjoyed playing jazz) was elected for a second term.

e)   A hurricane is a tropical storm that can do enormous damage.

5. **In defining clauses both** *that* **and** *which* **can be used with things.**

Toyota is a Japanese company *that/which* makes cars.

But for clauses that provide additional detail only *which* can be used:

Volkswagen, *which* is a German company, is a major car producer.

In defining clauses where the relative pronoun is the object its use is optional:

She applied to the university (*that/which*) her tutor had recommended.

The course (*that/which*) I wanted to take was not offered this semester.

The tutor (*who*) she wanted to meet was away for two months.

When the relative pronoun is the subject it must be included:

The scientists *who* discovered DNA worked in Cambridge.

Decide if the relative pronouns in the following are necessary. If not, cross them out.

a)   It was not known who was responsible for the explosion.

b)   The man who I read about was born in Scotland.

c)   The book that the professor wrote was remarkably short.

d)   Squirrels are mammals that live mainly in trees.

e)   The article that she referred to was published last year.

6. *Insert a suitable relative pronoun in the text below. Write* X *if the pronoun is optional.*

King Camp Gillette, a) . . . . invention of the disposable razor blade made his name world-famous, was an American b) . . . . had spent 40 years looking for a saleable invention. The idea c) . . . . changed his fortunes occurred in 1895, but he met considerable difficulties producing a thin, sharp blade d) . . . . could be made cheaply. He sold shares in the company to pay for the development work e). . . . . his partner, William Dickerson, was doing. In 1903, f) . . . . was their first year of business, they produced only 51 razors. But due to intensive advertising, g) . . . . potential Gillette quickly recognised, they rapidly increased sales to 250,000 two years later. The modern razor, h) . . . . is usually double-bladed, is directly related to the idea i) . . . . Gillette had over a hundred years ago.

18. Singular/Plural

1. **This can be a confusing area, but the following illustrate the main areas of difficulty:**

    a) Nouns should agree with verbs, and pronouns with nouns:

      Those problems are unique.

      There *are* many *arguments* in favour.

    b) Uncountable nouns and irregular plurals have no final -*s*:

      Most students receive free *tuition.*

      DNA is located in every part; *hair*, nails, *teeth* ...

    c) General statements normally use the plural:

      State *universities* have lower *fees.*

    d) *Each* and *every* are followed by singular nouns:

      Every *student* gets financial support.

    e) Two linked nouns should agree:

      Both the *similarities* and *differences* are important.

    Find the mistake in the following and decide what type (a–e above)
    it is.

    a) The proposal has both advantages and disadvantage.   (.....)
    b) A majority of children in Thailand is vaccinated against measles.   (.....)
    c) There are few young people in rural area.   (.....)
    d) Many places are experiencing an increase in crimes.   (.....)
    e) Each towns have their own councils.   (.....)

2. **Study the following group phrases.**

Singular + plural	Plural + plural	Plural + uncountable
half the universities	two types of institutions	three areas of enquiry
a range of businesses	various kinds of courses	several fields of research
one of the elements	many species of ants	rates of progress

Note that if a verb has more than one subject it must be plural, even if the preceding noun is singular:

Scores of students, some teachers and the president *are* at the meeting.

Their valuable suggestions and hard work *were* vital.

Certain group nouns, e.g. *team/army /government,* can be followed by either a singular or plural verb:

The team *was* defeated three times last month. (collectively)

The team *were* travelling by train or bus. (separately)

3. *Underline and correct the mistakes in the following (one per sentence).*

   a) More must be done to solve that problems of development.

   b) There are two sorts of college in Japan.

   c) The attitude towards this issue vary from person to person.

   d) Many culture from around the world are found in the city.

   e) In the country the people is more friendly.

   f) It is common to move from the countryside to find job.

   g) Huge number of cars use the motorway.

   h) The city have disadvantages such as a high rate of crime.

   i) Public transport lets us move to another places easily.

   j) There are bad pollution due to traffic congestion.

   k) People should not ignore important factors that affect their life.

4. *Read the text and choose the correct alternative.*

A large number of *company/companies has/have* developed *website/websites* in the last few years. Trading using the internet is called *e-commerce/e-commerces*, and *this/these is/are* divided into two main kinds: B2B and B2C. Many *business/businesses* want to use the internet to sell directly to *its/their* customers (B2C), but large numbers have experienced *trouble/troubles* with *security/securities* and other practical issues. In addition, the high start-up costs and the *expense/expenses* of advertising *means/mean* that *this/these* *company/companies* often struggle to make a profit.

19. Tenses

1. *Decide which tenses are used in the following examples (verbs in italic) and complete the table to explain why.*

a) According to Hoffman (1996), small firms *respond* more rapidly to changes …

b) Currently, inflation in the US *is rising* while imports *are falling*.

c) Since November there *has been* a significant increase in cases of influenza.

d) In the last three years more students *have been working* part-time.

e) After the war there *was* a sharp rise in divorce.

f) During 1998 they *were developing* a new system.

g) The study was published in June. It showed that in 1998 and 1999 profits *had increased* by 55%.

h) The forecast concludes that interest rates *will reach* 7.5% next year.

	Tense	Reason for use
a		
b		
c		
d		
e		
f		
g		
h		

NB. In the last month/year/decade = present perfect (unfinished period).
Last month/year/decade = simple past (finished period).

2. *Complete the following sentences by selecting the most suitable tenses.*

a) Home ownership.........................(rise) steadily for fifty years.

b) GM..........................(stand for) genetically modified.

c) Last year the police ....(record) a record number of crimes.

d) When she died in 1986 she ....(write) over 50 books.

e) By 2050 average temperatures ....(be) at least 2 degrees higher.

f) At the moment the bank ....(consider) a merger proposal from Barclays.

g) When the market crashed the company ....(build) 3 hotels in Asia.

h) Lee (1992) .... (dispute) Sakamoto's theory.

i) In the last six years inflation .... (fall) sharply in Europe.

3. **Simple or continuous?**

a) In general, the continuous is used to focus on the activity itself or to stress its temporary nature. Compare the following:

She has been writing that report for six days.	(activity)
He is writing a travel article.	(temporary)
She writes children's books.	(usually)

b) Also note that certain verbs are rarely used in the continuous. They are **state** verbs like *prefer*, *want* and *believe*. Another similar group is known as **performative** verbs (*assume, deny, promise, refuse, suggest*).

4. *Select either simple or continuous in each case:*

a) The team at Cambridge ....(work) on a rare type of brain disease.

b) He ....(believe) he will finish the study early next year.

c) This magazine ....(look for) a new writer on technology.

d) In the late 1990s she was working on rice plants but now she .... (research) potatoes.

e) The average age of marriage in Britain ....(rise) by six years since 1970.

f) The company .... (own) factories in 12 countries.

g) Most people in the city ....(live) within two kilometres of their work.

h) Dr McPherson ....(attend) a conference in South America this week.

cross reference

3.11   *Passives*
3.20   *Time Words and Phrases*

5. *When writing paragraphs, it is important to be clear about which time phrases control the tenses of verbs:*

For years, the condition of the family *has produced* some of the strongest debate heard in America. The statistics of collapse *have appeared* simple and clear. The proportion of children born outside marriage *rose* from 18% in *1980* to 33% in *1999*. The share of households made up of two parents and their children *fell* from 45% in *1960* to only 23% in *2000*.

In this case, the time phrase *For years* controls the tense of the first two sentences (present perfect). The following two sentences are in the simple past because of the dates *1980, 1999* and *1960,* which show finished periods.

6. *Read the text below and select the most suitable tense for each verb in brackets (time phrases in italic).*

For a long time gardeners a) . . . . (suspect) that using green fingers is just as effective as talking softly to plants to encourage growth. Scientists b) . . . . (develop) a robot that strokes young plants to make them grow stronger and faster. *But after research a year ago* c) . . . . (confirm) that plants need the human touch, scientists at Greenwich University d) . . . . (develop) the stroking machine they call Dr Green.

Dr Green e) . . . . (be display) *at the last Chelsea Flower Show*, where it f) . . . . (demonstrate) the technique of brushing the tips of young plants to produce stronger specimens. David Carey, who is leading the research, g) . . . . (say) that the machine could avoid the use of chemicals.

Currently, Dr Green h) . . . . (be test) on a large scale by a commercial grower. Stroking plants once a day i) . . . . (make) them 30% stronger, which is what you need before you plant them out. *When another kind of plant was stroked* once a week, it j) . . . . (develop) increased insect resistance. The research team hope that a cheap version of Dr Green k) . . . . (be available) to amateur gardeners *by 2007*.

20. Time Words and Phrases

1. **Study the use of the following:**

   She went on a training course *for* six weeks. (with numbers)

   The report must be finished *by* June 12th. (on or before)

   He has been president *since* 1998. (usually with present perfect)

   They are studying in Bristol *until* March. (end of a period)

   The library was opened two years *ago.* (usually with past)

   The hotel is closed *during* the winter. (with noun)

   Before writing he studied over 100 sources. (often followed by *-ing* form; also *after*)

cross reference
3.5 *Conjunctions*
3.19 *Tenses*

2. **Compare the use of the following phrases.**

   Recently, there has been a sharp rise in internet use. (present perfect)

   Currently, there is a vigorous debate about human rights. (present)

   Last year there was an election in Spain. (past)

   In the last year there has been a sharp rise in inflation. (present perfect)

3. *Study Rachel's schedule for her last business trip and complete the sentences below with a suitable word. It is now April 16.*

March 12	Fly London – Milan
March 13–14	Conference Milan
March 15	Train Milan – Paris
March 16	Meeting in Paris office
March 17	Fly Paris – Hong Kong
March 18–19	Tour of new development
March 20	Fly Hong Kong – London

   a)   .... month Rachel made a business trip.

   b)   .... her trip she visited three countries.

   c)   .... March 18th she had travelled 10,000 miles.

   d)   She was away from home .... nine days altogether.

   e)   A month .... she was in Paris.

   f)   She stayed in Hong Kong .... March 20th.

   g)   .... she is writing a report on her trip.

4. *Choose the best alternative in each case.*

   a)   *Currently/recently* she has been researching the life cycle of a species of wasp.

   b)   She lived in France *until/during* the war broke out, and then she went home.

   c)   Professor Yung has worked here *since/for* sixteen years.

   d)   *Last month/in the last month* a new book was published on the subject.

   e)   Applications must be received *by/on* November 25th.

f)   *Since/during* her arrival last May she has re-organised the department.

g)   *During/for* the winter most farmers in the region find work in the towns.

5. *Complete the following text with a suitable word or phrase.*

EATING OUT

a) . . . . the last few decades there has been a significant change in eating habits in the UK. b) . . . . the early 1980s eating out in restaurants and cafes has increased steadily. There are several reasons for this trend.

50 years c) . . . . most women were housewives, and cooked for their families every day. But d) . . . . , with more women working outside the home, less time has been available for food preparation. e) . . . . , 71% of women aged 20–45 are at work, and f) . . . . 2015 it is estimated that this will rise to 84%.

Another factor is the growth in disposable income, which has risen significantly g) . . . . the late 1970s. With more money in their pockets people are more likely to save the trouble of shopping and cooking by visiting their local restaurant.

6. *Study the details of Napoleon's life and complete the biography below.*

1769	born in Corsica
1784	entered military school in Paris
1789	French revolution started
1793	promoted to brigadier general
1796	appointed to command army of Italy; married Josephine
1799	returned from Egypt and became First Consul of France
1807	France controlled most of continental Europe
1810	divorced Josephine and married Marie-Louise, daughter of Austrian emperor
1812	forced to retreat from Russia
1814	exiled to Elba
1815	defeated at Waterloo and exiled to St Helena
1821	died in exile

Napoleon entered military school at the age of 15, five years a) . . . . the start of the French revolution. He rose quickly, becoming brigadier general at 24 and commander of the Italian army three years b) . . . . At 30 he was effectively the French dictator, and due to his military genius France controlled most of Europe c) . . . . 1807. When he divorced his first wife, Josephine, in 1810, they had been married d) . . . . 14 years. His campaigns were successful e) . . . . 1812, but in that year the disastrous retreat from Moscow marked the start of his decline. However, f) . . . . his years of absolute power he had made significant changes to European law and government. Although he died nearly 200 years g) . . . . , Napoleon's influence is still felt throughout the continent.

4. Writing Models

Student Introduction

There are many possible formats for different types of essays, as well as non-academic texts such as letters and CVs. If a selection of formal letters, for example, is studied, it will be seen that different styles of heading and layout are used by different organisations. However, the following models are provided so that students may use the outlines confident that they will be acceptable in almost all situations.

Comparison and argument are common components of essay titles, and the models given here show one way of answering the questions. However, it must be remembered that argument may be only one part of the question, so that both comparison and discussion (plus other elements) could well be needed in the same essay (as illustrated in 4.4 *Comparison Essay*).

Faculties and departments may well give new students guidance about what is required in terms of style and layout. Above all, students need to examine a variety of styles of letters, CVs and essays, and to develop a suitable style of their own by synthesising the most appropriate features.

1. Formal Letters

cross reference

3.1 Abbreviations
4.2 CVs

1. *You have applied for a place on an MA course at a British university. This is the letter you have received in reply:*

---

a)   **Arts & Social Sciences Admissions Office**
                          Wye House
                        Central Campus
                  University of Borchester
                     Borchester BR3 5HT
                      United Kingdom

b) Ms P Tan
    54 Sydney Road
    Rowborough RB1 6FD

c) Ref: MB/373

d) 3 May 2002

e) Dear Ms Tan

f) *Application for MA International Studies*

g) Further to your recent application, I would like to invite you to the university for an informal interview on Tuesday 21st May at 11 am. You will be able to meet the course supervisor, Dr Schmidt, and look round the department.

h) A map of the campus and instructions for finding the university are enclosed.

i) Please let me know if you will be able to attend on the date given.

j) Yours sincerely

k) *M. Bramble*

l) Mick Bramble
    Administrative Assistant
    Arts & Social Sciences

Enc.

Label the following features of formal letters with the letters (a–l) from the left margin above.

(*d*) Date	(...) Ending	(...) Request for response
(...) Greeting	(...) Address of recipient	(...) Address of sender
(...) Further details	(...) Reason for writing	(...) Sender's reference
(...) Subject headline	(...) Signature	(...) Writer's name and title

Note the following points:

a) When writing to somebody whose name you do not know, e.g. The Manager, use *Dear Sir* and *Yours faithfully*.

b) A formal letter generally uses the family name in the greeting (*Dear Ms Tan*). Certain organisations may, however, use a first name with a family name or even a first name alone (*Dear Jane Tan/Dear Jane*).

c) If the sender includes a reference it is helpful to quote it in your reply.

2. *Write a reply to Mr Bramble making the following points:*

   a) You will attend the interview on the date given.

   b) You would like to have the interview one hour later, owing to train times.

54 Sydney Road
Rowborough
RB1 6FD

3. *Study the following newspaper advert. You have decided to apply for this job. Make notes for your letter of application, then write the letter, paying attention to layout as well as content.*

STAFF REQUIRED FOR RECEPTION WORK AT CITY HOTEL

We are looking for enthusiastic and helpful receptionists (m/f) to join our team. Candidates should be well-presented and able to speak at least two languages. Hotel experience not necessary as training will be given. Ability to get on with people and work in a team more important. Some evening and weekend work. Good conditions and rates of pay. Apply in writing with CV and covering letter to: The Manager, Hotel Nelson, Queens Road, Rowborough RB2 4RN quoting Ref. EN2.

2. CVs

1. **CV stands for** *curriculum vitae* **(also known as a** *resumé***).**

   A CV is a summary of your education and work experience, often requested by prospective employers. Most professionals store their CVs electronically so that they can be updated when necessary.

2. **There is considerable debate about the format of CVs, and much depends on your experience and the area you are working in.**

   The example given below is relatively short, as would be expected for a recent graduate.

Sarah Ann Atkins

DOB 19.6.77

Email: saa@virgin.net

Career aim

To develop my experience in marketing in a senior managerial role, using my knowledge of European languages.

Career history

2001–present	**Marketing Assistant, Eastern Foods, Derby**
	In my current post I am part of a team involved in marketing our products throughout the UK. I have helped organise several campaigns and given presentations in connection with these.
1997–8	**English Teacher, Montpellier, France**
	During my year abroad I taught English at a school in Montpellier, which not only helped strengthen my French but also gave me valuable lessons in self-reliance.

Academic qualifications

2001	**MBA** (Rowborough University Business School)
2000	**BA** (Hons) 2:1 in European Languages (University of Leeds) with distinction in spoken French

Skills

Languages:	knowledge of Spanish & French (advanced)/Italian (good)
ICT:	competence with the following applications:
	Word
	Excel
	Groupwise

Personal

I would describe myself as outgoing, friendly and a good communicator. I apply these qualities to establishing good customer relations and working with colleagues as part of a team.

Note:

a) The above format is only one possibility and it is worth looking at other CVs to compare layouts.

b) Your address and phone number should be in your covering letter, not on the CV.

c) List qualifications and experience in reverse chronological order, starting with the most recent. Prospective employers are mainly interested in your latest achievements.

d) Do not clutter the CV with details of hobbies that are irrelevant to the job you are applying for. Similarly, your early education is unimportant.

e) Do not just give job titles but explain in detail what you did.

f) Give references only if asked to do so.

3. *Prepare a CV for yourself. First make notes of all the important information (with dates), using similar headings to those in the example above. Then organise it as clearly as possible. Finally, type it on a computer and store it so it can be updated in future.*

3.   Designing and Reporting Surveys

1. **Surveys, in which people are asked questions about their opinions or behaviour, are a common feature of academic work, especially in fields such as education, psychology and social sciences.**

   What are the reasons for carrying out surveys? List your ideas below.

   a)

   b)

   c)

2. *Study the report of a survey carried out on a university campus. Complete the report by inserting suitable words from the box below into the gaps.*

sample	conducted	slightly	respondents	random
questions	majority	questioned	mentioned	interviewees
common	questionnaire	generally	minority	

   Introduction

   A survey was a) ....to find out how part-time work affects student life and study. The research was done by asking students selected at b) ....on the campus to complete a c) ....(see Appendix 1). 50 students were d) .... on Saturday April 23rd, with approximately equal numbers of male and female students.

   Findings

   Of the e) ...., 30% currently had part-time jobs, 20% had had part-time jobs, but half had never done any work during university semesters (see Table 1). f) ....who were working or who had worked were next asked about the reasons for taking the jobs. The most common reason was lack of money (56%), but many students said that they found the work useful experience (32%) and others g) ....social benefits (12%).

   Table 1. Do you have or have you had a part-time job?

	Men	Women	Total	%
have job now	8	7	15	30
had job before	4	6	10	20
never had job	14	11	25	50

   The 25 students with work experience were next asked about the effects of the work on their studies. A significant h) .... (64%) claimed that there were no negative effects at all. However, 24% said that their academic work suffered i) ...., while a small j) .... (12%) reported serious adverse results, such as tiredness in lectures and falling marks.

   Further k) .... examined the nature of the work that the students did. The variety of jobs was surprising, from van driver to busker, but the most l) .... areas were catering and bar work (44%) and secretarial (32%). Most students worked between 10 and 15 hours per week, though two (8%) worked over 25 hours. Rates of pay were m) .... near the national minimum wage, and averaged £5.20 per hour.

The final question invited students to comment on their experience of part-time work. Many (44%) made the point that students should be given larger grants so that they could concentrate on their studies full-time, but others felt that they gained something from the experience, such as meeting new people and getting insights into various work environments. One student said that she had met her current boyfriend while working in a city centre restaurant.

Conclusions

It is clear that part-time work is now a common aspect of student life. Many students find jobs at some point in their studies, but an overwhelming majority (88%) of those deny that it has a damaging effect on their studies. Most students work for only 2–3 hours per day on average, and a significant number claim some positive results from their employment.

Obviously, our survey was limited to a relatively small n) .... by time constraints, and a fuller study might modify our findings in various ways.

3. *Question 1 is given above Table 1. What were the other questions in this survey? Using the results above, write possible questions below.*
   2.
   3.
   4.
   5.
   6.
   7.

4. *What is the main tense in (a)* **Introduction** *and* **Findings** *and (b)* **Conclusion***? Explain the reason for the difference.*

5. **Questionnaire Design.**
   Which is the better question?
   i)   How old are you?
   ii) Are you (a) under 20, (b) between 21 and 30, (c) over 30?

6. *What is the main difference between the two questions?*
   i)   What do you think of university students?
   ii) Do you think university students are (a) lazy, (b) hardworking, (c) average

7. *You are preparing a survey on one of the following subjects. Prepare a questionnaire of no more than ten questions to collect the most useful data.*
   a) How overseas students learn vocabulary
   b) Student attitudes to the cinema
   c) A comparison of undergraduate and post-graduate leisure activities

4. Comparison Essay

A COMPARISON OF CLASSROOM LEARNING WITH INTERNET-BASED TEACHING

Introduction

Since the late 1990s internet-based teaching (also known as e-education) has emerged as a potential rival to traditional classroom learning. The former normally involves having access to a secure site on the internet where a graded series of lessons is available, which have assignments sent and returned by email. Although online courses are now offered by many institutions, it is by no means clear that they offer real advantages compared with classroom education. Little research has been done so far on their effectiveness, but this essay sets out to examine the arguments on both sides and attempts to draw conclusions from them.

The benefits of online study

Two main advantages of internet use in education are put forward. Firstly, it is seen as more economical, in that once a course is prepared, it can be used by large numbers of students. The savings made by not having to employ so many teachers should be reflected in cheaper course fees. The second benefit is convenience; instead of having to attend classes at fixed times and places, students are free to study when they choose and progress at their own pace. Furthermore, in studying from home there is no need to travel to the college or university, which saves both time and money. A student living in a small town in China, for example, can now study a course at an American college without the worry of travelling, accommodation or homesickness.

The continuing popularity of classroom education

Despite the considerations mentioned above, classroom learning shows no signs of being replaced by e-learning. It seems that face-to-face contact with a teacher is still regarded as the best way for students to make progress, despite the expense and inconvenience involved. Not only the personal contact with a teacher but also the support and encouragement gained from being part of a class may be reasons for this. Membership of a group may also create a useful spirit of competition, which stimulates learning.

Discussion

Given the increasing pressure on university places in many countries, internet-based teaching is widely seen as a convenient development. However, e-learning eliminates personal contact and travel from education, which are possibly the aspects many students value. Sitting at home working on a computer may be economical, but clearly cannot replace the social experience of attending courses. However, there are many people who are unable, through either work or family commitments, or owing to lack of funds, to go to classes, and who would clearly find internet learning beneficial. Online courses can also be used to support taught courses, for instance by providing access to extra materials. In many ways these kinds of courses are similar to 'universities of the air', such as Britain's Open University, which have developed distance learning so successfully in the last forty years.

Conclusion

Faced by growing demand for university places, many institutions are likely to develop online courses, but the apparent benefits of e-learning may be less than first appear. Students seem to value the personal contact of the classroom highly, despite its cost and inconvenience. There may be a role for internet-based courses to supplement teacher-taught ones, and certainly for people with other commitments they will be the only practical option. There is an urgent need for research on the effectiveness of this type of learning, which should help maximise its advantages in the future.

(Approximately 550 words)

cross reference

2.1   *Cause and Effect*
2.3   *Comparisons*
2.4   *Definitions*
2.6   *Examples*
2.7   *Generalisations*
2.11 *Synonyms*

Read the essay carefully and find:

a) a definition

b) an example

c) a generalisation

d) a phrase expressing cause and effect

e) a passive

f) a phrase expressing caution

g) three synonyms for *internet-based teaching*

5. Discursive Essay

EDUCATION IS THE MOST IMPORTANT FACTOR IN NATIONAL DEVELOPMENT – DISCUSS

Introduction

'National development' is a rather vague term that could mean the growth of a sense of national identity, or the development of a country's economy. This essay will use the second definition, since this is more commonly seen as a function of education provided by the state. Many European countries, such as Germany, began providing primary education for all in the late nineteenth century, in the phase of early industrialisation.

Education must be considered on several different levels, so that today most western countries are concerned with provision from nursery to higher education, whereas developing countries attempt to deliver basic education (e.g. reading and writing) to their people.

This paper attempts to evaluate the importance of these varying levels of educational provision in encouraging economic growth, compared with other factors such as national culture, natural resources and government. The role of education in fostering development will be examined first, and then other factors that affect growth will be considered.

The impact of education

At its simplest, education sets out to teach literacy and numeracy. People who can read and count are capable of being trained for many roles in the industrial or service sectors, as well as learning by themselves. Even in the simplest economies, dependent on agriculture, the education of women has been shown to lead to dramatic improvements in family welfare. In more developed economies further skills are required, such as languages, engineering and computing. Good education does not merely teach people how to function passively, but provides them with the skills to ask questions and therefore make improvements. At university level, education is closely involved in research that leads to technical and social advances.

The limits of education

Education does not operate in a vacuum: cultural, religious, legal and other factors all influence the rate of economic growth. Soviet Russia, for example, had an advanced educational system, but many graduates were under-employed owing to the restrictions of the political system. Similar situations exist in many countries today because of the failure of the economy to expand fast enough to create sufficient jobs. Clearly, then, development requires efficient and honest government to encourage a dynamic economy.

A strong work ethic, as found in the USA, Japan and Germany, also aids growth. In such societies children are brought up to believe that both the individual and society will benefit from hard work. Natural resources such as oil are another consideration. Brunei, for example, previously a poor country reliant on fishing, today has one of the highest per capita GDPs in the world.

Discussion and conclusion

Education alone may have little effect on a nation's development. The world's first industrial revolution, for instance, occurred in eighteenth-century Britain, when the majority of people were still illiterate (some pioneer industrialists themselves could not read or write). It seems that the availability of capital and a secure political and legal environment were more crucial in this case.

However, given the presence of some of the factors mentioned in the previous section, education clearly has an important part to play in developing the skills and abilities of the people. Ultimately, they are the most important resource a country possesses, and their education is a priority for all successful states.

(Approximately 550 words)

Read the essay carefully and then analyse the introduction by completing the table below using categories from the box.

Example   Definition 2   Outline   Topic   Definition 1   Reason

Sentence	Type	
1		'National development' is a rather …
2		This essay will use the second …
3		Many European countries, such as …
4		Education must be considered …
5		This paper attempts to evaluate …
6		The role of education in …

Writing Tests

These tests can be used to assess different aspects of writing performance. The first test assesses cohesion. The accuracy tests (2 and 3) check use of particular word classes such as conjunctions or prepositions. Students having difficulties with, for example, articles, should look at the relevant unit in Part 3. Test 4 is a comparison. They can be used in the classroom or for self-assessment.

WRITING TEST 1

(Cohesion)

The parts of sentences below make two paragraphs that compare speaking with writing. Some parts are already numbered. Fill in the remaining numbers. Use internal clues and punctuation to help you find the correct order.

SPEAKING AND WRITING

1)   When we speak, it is normally to one or

…) to study our listeners' faces for expressions that tell

…) for example agreement, or amusement.

…) they often find the situation stressful.

3)   As we speak, we are able

…) For most people, speaking feels like a natural activity,

…) a small number of people, who are often well known to us.

…) If their expressions show incomprehension

…) us their reaction to what we are saying;

…) though if they have to make a formal speech

…) we will probably restate what we are saying.

…) Writers cannot check if the readers understand, or are interested

…) to avoid the dangers of being misunderstood by readers,

…) who cannot look puzzled to

1) Writing, however, is much more like speaking to

…) Unless we are writing a letter to a friend

…) This is the reason why writing is more difficult than

…) make the writer explain what he means again.

…) in what they are writing.

…) we have no way of knowing who may read our words.

…) It also explains why writing must be as clear and simple as possible,

…) speaking, and often uses a more formal style.

…) an unknown audience.

WRITING TEST 2

(Accuracy)

Read the text for gist and then complete it by writing **one** *word in each gap.*

Most overseas students who come to study (a) .... English-speaking countries find that their first (b) .... is listening. Understanding (c) .... many forms of spoken English is more (d) .... than they expected.

(e) ...., after a month (f) .... two, the majority find that their listening (g) ...., and their next concern is speaking. This skill is more difficult to practise, so improvement (h) .... to be slower. But (i) .... three or four months most students find that (j) .... can function quite (k) .... in terms of shopping and travelling.

A (l) .... area of difficulty is writing, which is possibly the (m) .... difficult skill to master, (n) .... it is more impersonal than oral / aural skills and depends (o) .... the student learning a complex series of conventions. This explains (p) .... many students find it (q) .... to attend (r) .... intensive course in academic English (s) .... they begin (t) .... university studies.

(WRITING TEST 3

(Accuracy)

Read the text for gist and then complete it by writing **one** *word in each gap.*

All students need a) .... to live, so finding a suitable place is likely to be a priority when they arrive to start a new course. Apart b) .... the minority c) .... live with their parents, there are only two d) .... of accommodation which are generally affordable.

e) .... all universities provide f) .... of residence, which can help new students g) .... friends and develop a social life. They can be a h) .... choice, usually being close to other university facilities, i) .... some may find that they are noisy, expensive and have j) .... small rooms.

The alternative is to rent k) .... house or flat from a private landlord with a group of other students. l) .... kind of shared accommodation m) .... offer greater independence and privacy, and can n) .... be more economical. However, it does mean taking o) .... more responsibility, p) .... bills need paying and the rooms have to q) .... cleaned.

Wherever students choose to live, several things are r) .... A quiet place to work, a sense of security and s) .... environment that allows t) .... to sleep properly all contribute to academic success.

WRITING TEST 4

(Comparison)

Study the information in the table comparing two cities, which both have good universities. Use it to write a report on which would be the more suitable location for an overseas student planning a one-year course (about 200 words).

	Borchester	Rowborough
population	220,000	1,560,000
summer climate	warm and wet	cool and quite dry
winter climate	cool and windy	cold and wet
city type	old cathedral city with modern service industries	19th century industrial city with modern mixed industries
terrain	flat, lots of parks	hilly with several lakes
cost of accommodation	quite high	medium
public transport	bus service not very good	buses and trams, both good
main advantages	relaxed atmosphere	good range of shops and sports facilities
main drawbacks	university campus is 6 km from city centre	high rates of crime in some areas
distance from capital	230 km	125 km

Answers

Providing answers for a writing course is less clear cut than for other language areas. In some exercises there is only one possible answer, but in other cases several possibilities exist. Teachers need to exercise common sense, and accept any reasonable answer. In the case of exercises where students can choose their own topic and it is therefore impossible to provide an answer, students still appreciate having a model answer, and so some have been included.

Part 1: The Writing Process

1. **Background to Writing**

    1

notes	to record reading or lectures	
report	to describe something a student has conducted, e.g. an experiment/a survey	1000–2000
project	research conducted either individually or in a group on subject chosen by student(s)	1000–3000
essay	piece of writing used to assess coursework/ subject chosen by teacher	1000–5000
thesis/dissertation	long piece of writing on subject chosen by student for final assessment in Master's/ PhD course	30,000–70,000
article/paper	writing published in academic journal	5000–10,000

    2bi   abstract
    2bii   acknowledgements
    2biii appendix
    2biv   bibliography
    2bv   case study
    2bvi   preface
    2bvii index

    4a   title
    4b   sub-heading
    4c   phrase
    4d   sentence
    4e   paragraph

5   Texts are divided into paragraphs to separate the main points and make them easier to read. Paragraphs usually vary in length from three to eight sentences.

para 2 begins:	The first issue to …
para 3 begins:	Diversification must also …
para 4 begins:	A further consideration …

2.   Developing Plans from Titles

1a	Define	give a definition
	Outline	describe the main features
1b	Compare	examine the similarities
	Contrast	look at the differences
1c	Evaluate	consider the value
1d	Trace	describe the main features
	Illustrate	give examples
2	Describe	give a detailed account
	Examine	divide into sections and discuss each critically
	State	give a clear and simple account
	Suggest	make a proposal and support it
	Summarise	deal with a complex subject by giving the main points

4   Sample plan:

title	Evaluate the effects of mergers in the motor industry in the last ten years
introduction	definition of *merger*
	background to motor industry
	outline of essay
main body	case studies of two mergers
	discussion of benefits of each merger
conclusion	summary of findings: value of mergers depends on quality of management in merged firm

5   The following sections are the most important:

5a   An analysis of candidates for membership before 2010/An outline of the enlargement of the EU between 1975 and the present.

5b   A study of major privatisations in the UK/A discussion of the benefits achieved by privatisation.

5c A report on the spread of TB worldwide/A case study showing how TB relates to social class.

5d A report on the development of children who remain at home until five/A discussion comparing speaking ability in both groups of children.

5e The benefits of using books/The drawbacks of internet sources.

6a *Identify* means to select and explain. The writer must identify the chief reasons for poverty in the Chinese countryside.

6b *Calculate* means to make a mathematical estimate. Here the writer must look at patterns of coffee consumption and attempt to calculate how much difference a price decrease would make.

6c *Classify* means to put into categories. Different types of desert need to be described, and then methods of control should be proposed.

3. **Evaluating a Text**

2

a	fact	true
b	fact	false
c	opinion	
d	fact	true
e	fact & opinion	true
f	fact	false
g	fact & opinion	false

5a Factual until last sentence (*In the future …*), which is an opinion.

5b Most sentences mix facts and opinions. Most of the facts are untrue, e.g. the population is not two million. Clearly an unreliable source!

5c Mainly opinion, supported by some facts at the end. Evaluation depends on judging how well the writer builds his/her case. Subject knowledge clearly necessary.

5d Although this begins with a generally accepted fact, the second sentence contains a totally untrue statement, and the speculation built on this is absurd.

5e Mainly factual, except for an opinion in the first sentence (*shocking*). The final sentence is speculation.

4. **Understanding Purpose and Register**

2a amuse/entertain

2b inform/persuade

2c inform

5

a	formal	without recourse/empowered/the complainant
b	academic	yielded clear interactions/review of the literature/Pearson and Mayer (1998)
c	journalistic	Amazing recent research/old folk/'grey entrepreneurs'

5. Selecting Key Points

2   Many possibilities, but should include the idea of financial success and medical developments, e.g. *Millionaire American medical inventor.*

3   1) b   2) a   3) c

4.1 Lord May… has claimed that the world is facing a wave of extinctions similar to the five mass extinctions of past ages.

4.2 He calculates that the current rate of extinction is between 100 and 1000 times faster than the historical average.

4.3 … the present situation is caused by human consumption of plants, which has resulted in a steady increase in agriculture and a consequent reduction in habitat for animals.

4.4 Lord May also pointed out that it was very difficult to make accurate estimates as nobody knew how many species of animals lived on the planet.

5a   …bottled water costs 700 times more than tap water, but is often of inferior quality.

… although bottled water advertising often associated the product with sport and health there was no truth in this link.

Labels on bottled water often referred to 'spring' and 'natural water', which were meaningless phrases.

5b   Now the genetic code of the plague bacterium has been 'read' successfully by scientists; a total of 465 million 'letters' of DNA. They believe that this will help in the development of vaccines for the plague …

6. Note-Making

1   to keep a record of reading/lectures

to revise for exams

to help remember main points

to prepare for essays

2   Before: listening/reading/selecting

After: writing/speaking

5. Source: Nemecova, I. (1998) *Medical Report* 34, pp. 78–86

    Malaria increasing esp. resistant strains

    350m.+ cases p.a. (4 × level 1970s)

    Causes: a)   increase in poverty > less money for sanitation

    　　　　 b)   increased travel (migrants/tourists)

    　　　　 c)   overuse of antibiotics

    Vaccine? – difficult because of different strains but in trials

6. Source: Pitnam, E.B. (1993) *Volcanic Disasters* 221

    1815　　　　Mt Tambora (Indonesia) exploded

    　　　　　　100 km³ debris ⟋ atmosphere ⟶ affected
    weather around world

    1816　　　　NE USA & Europe cold summers destroyed harvests >
    prices rose > more emigrants to west of USA

7. **Paraphrasing**

    2   (b) is the better paraphrase (in (a) *changes in the weather* and *the region to the south* are not as precise as *a long dry period* and *the mountains at the river's source*).

    4   A number of possibilities are acceptable here. These are suggestions.

    4b   discovered/visualising an attractive view/encourage/rapidly

    4c   scientists/split

    4d   was asked to think of/attempted

    5b   The findings showed that the group thinking of waterfalls fell asleep 20 minutes quicker.

    5c   It appears that mechanical tasks like counting sheep are too boring to make people sleepy.

    6b   It is thought that about one in ten people suffer from severe insomnia.

    6c   The cost of insomnia for the American economy has been calculated at approximately $35 billion a year.

    7   Again, there is a range of possibilities, of which the following is an example:

    Findings by sleep researchers suggest that established cures for insomnia, for instance counting sheep, do not work, though visualising an attractive view may significantly encourage sleep. 50 insomniacs were split into three groups by Oxford university scientists. The first thought of water falling, and the second attempted to count sheep. A third group was not specially instructed. The findings show that the group thinking of waterfalls went to sleep faster. It appears that repetitive situations are not effective, because they are too tedious. The research has multiple uses, since 10% of the population are believed to have difficulty sleeping, and the cost of insomnia for the American economy has been calculated at around $35 billion annually.

8   Sample paraphrase:

Antarctica was unexplored until the 20th century, and still has a tiny population in relation to its size. Yet it suffers from various pollution problems which have been described in a report by a New Zealand government agency. The low temperatures there impede the usual pattern of decay, though compared with most parts of the world it remains in pristine condition. Some long-established scientific bases have large piles of garbage around them.

Few people realise that Antarctica has very little precipitation, so that in the current context of global warming the ice tends to reveal the rubbish that previously was slowly being buried under snow. For more than a decade the nations involved in Antarctic research have respected an agreement to repatriate their garbage, and this should gradually solve the problem. But there are a few items that will not be cleared up, since they belonged to the early period of exploration and have now acquired historic interest.

8.   Summary Writing

1   Features of good summaries should include: selection of main features/accuracy (i.e. not distorting the original)/clear expression.

2   making detailed notes from sections of journal articles and books
making global summaries of writers' ideas and theses

3   Possible answers:

3b   key points/main ideas

3c   use your own words/paraphrase

3d   order of the ideas where necessary

3e   important points/ideas

4   a)   is the best summary

b)   fails to describe the experiment

c)   neither describes the experiment or its significance

6   Possible answers:

6a   weather forecasting methods

6b   blossoming of local tree

6c   castor (for dry)

6d   the monsoon can be quite accurately forecast by the time of the tree's flowering

7   Model answer:

Indian scientists are checking ancient weather forecasting methods, such as the old saying that links the date of the monsoon to the flowering time of a local tree. This has been used by farmers to select either peanuts (for wet conditions) or castor (for dry). Dr Kanani of Gujarat Agricultural University has found that the monsoon can be quite accurately forecast using the time of the tree's flowering.

8   Model answer:

Recent Indian research confirms the accuracy of an ancient method of forecasting the monsoon's arrival used by farmers to choose crops.

9.   Combining Sources

1a   4

1b   to introduce summaries

1c   Others, however,

3a   direct quote: 'such procedures are now labelled "interfering with nature"'

summary: GM techniques are no different from breeding techniques that have been practised by humans for thousands of years.

3b   On the other hand

3c   Source A states that

Source B considers that

He believes that

4   Model answer:

Source C claims that tourism creates a significant amount of employment which provides a welcome alternative to traditional work such as farming. However, Source D points out that many of these jobs are insecure and poorly paid, being likely to contribute to social tensions. This negative view is partly supported by Source E, who insists that despite some positive examples the more common experience of developing countries is for tourism to exacerbate social ills such as crime and prostitution.

10.   Planning a Text

1   Other possible ideas:

tourism helps poorer countries develop

tourist industry vulnerable to political/natural disasters

package holidays helped to popularise foreign travel

huge potential demand from developing countries

2   Most suitable structure would be based on time, since the title asks for study of past and predictions for the future.

3   Sample plan:
Main body:
ii)   package holidays helped to popularise foreign travel
iii) tourism helped poorer countries to develop
iv)   constant demand for new destinations and new types of holiday

Conclusion: there is a huge potential demand for travel in developing countries but tourist industry is vulnerable to political/natural disasters

4a   For and against
4b   Comparison
4c   Time
4d   For and against
4e   Comparison

5   Main body:
i)   benefits of TV advertising: reach large audience, have strong impact
ii)   drawbacks: expensive and can be ignored
iii) benefits of newspaper advertising: flexible, cheap, focused
iv)   drawbacks: static

Conclusion: TV more effective in reaching large numbers but newspapers probably better for specialised markets

7   It would be better to include (a), (c) and (e) in the introduction as background information. (b), (d) and (f) would contribute to the main body. A discussion/conclusion section is needed to assess the overall situation. A revised plan might look like this:

Introduction	background
	outline of essay
Main body	reasons for using private sector
	negative effects on state system
	positive effects on state system
	discussion
Conclusion	summary of argument

11. Organising Paragraphs

3.1 Topic
3.2 Definition
3.3 Example

3.4 Detail

3.5 Detail

3.6 Reason

4   Topic: London has been …

    Restatement: For many centuries …

    Reason: Its dominance is due to

    Detail: 500 years ago …

5.1 Topic: The new Leisure …

5.2 Detail: Mark Roberts …

5.3 Detail: The opening has …

5.4 Reason: This was because …

5.5 Detail: The architects …

6.1 … was developed in the 19th century.

6.2 … to isolate, punish and reform.

6.3 … there has been a steep rise in the number of prisoners.

6.4 … as being 'universities of crime'.

6.5 … how effective prisons are today.

7.1 Prisons appear to offer society three benefits.

7.2 Firstly, they punish prisoners by depriving them of freedom.

7.3 In addition, offenders are segregated from society so they cannot commit further crimes.

7.4 Finally, they offer the possibility of reform through training programmes.

8.1 Topic: Prisons, however, appear to many observers to be failing in the 21st century.

8.2 Detail: In many countries the prison population is rising steadily.

8.3 Detail: Furthermore, many prisoners return to prison after their release; they are repeat offenders.

8.4 Reason: This suggests that few prisons offer effective reform programmes.

8.5 Detail: In addition, prison conditions can often be brutal and degrading.

12. Organising the Main Body

2   Order & titles:

2.1 Methods (b)

2.2 Findings (d)

2.3 Case study (c)

2.4 Discussion (a)

3a   For and against/type 1

3b   Comparison

4   (Some variation possible.)

4a   1.   factories originally sited to make use of water power (in 18th C.)
     2.   in nineteenth century factories built near canals/railways for access to markets
     3.   first factories employed unskilled workers; often women and children
     4.   early employers enforced strict codes of discipline
     5.   workers forced to adopt a regular timetable to maintain production
     6.   later some employers offered social benefits, e.g. housing/education

4b   1.   many older students have lost interest in learning and disrupt classes
     2.   problem students waste everybody's time, including their own
     3.   some students more suited to work that doesn't require qualifications
     4.   in future, almost all jobs will require academic skills
     5.   if they left at 14, students would be unlikely to find proper jobs
     6.   effort should be made in primary schools to prevent pupils falling behind

6   Possible answers:

     Para 2   The main factor
              In the first place
              Then
              Finally,

     Para 3   Turning to the subject of
              The first point is that
              Secondly
              Lastly,

     Para 4   Another important area
              Firstly
              In addition

13. Introductions

1   optional: a/c
     usual: d/e/g

7a   v

7b   i

7c   iv

7d   vi

7e   ii

7f   iii

9a   Higher Education

9b   depending on country chosen, recent developments/debate on HE could be mentioned

9c   reference could be made to rising student numbers/debate about costs (who should pay)/value of research for economic development

9d   essay could focus geographically on one or two countries, either similar or different economically

historically the discussion could be limited to the past ten/twenty/fifty years

9e   plan will depend on decisions made in (c) above

10   Model answer:

The last two decades have seen a steady increase in demand for higher (i.e. university-level) education worldwide. Rising costs in this sector have put pressure on national budgets, causing many countries to attempt to shift some of the cost to the students, often in the form of loans. A degree generally remains the key to better jobs and opportunities, yet if students have to pay a greater share of the cost this will discriminate against poorer families. This essay examines the question of access to university by comparing the situation in a developed country, the United States, with a developing country, Turkey.

14. Conclusions

1a   ii

1b   iii

1c   v

1d   iv

1e   ii

1f   i

1g   ii

1h   iv

2   Neither conclusion is complete – synthesis is required.

2a   Summary of discussion

2b   Limitations of study/proposals for future research

3   Suggested order (variations possible):
Summary of main findings

Reference to comparative studies *or* implications of findings

Limitations of research

Proposals for further research

4 Model answer:

Summary: The results suggest that culture was only one factor in determining successful adaptation. Older students, those with previous experience of living abroad, and those with better language proficiency all seemed to adapt better.

Implications: The findings suggest that students should possibly study abroad when they are more mature, and that they should aim for a higher level of language ability before they leave home.

Limitations: Although this was quite a large survey only about 30% of overseas students at the university were involved. Some national groups were under-represented.

Proposals. As we are not aware of other previous research in this field, it would be useful to replicate the study in another university, possibly with a different cross-section of overseas students, to see if similar results emerged.

15. Re-reading and Re-writing

4 Model answer:

Despite this, there are significant differences between the structure and workings of the higher education system in the two countries. This essay attempts to compare the admission procedures, length of courses for first and higher degrees, teaching methods, assessment procedures and systems of financial support for students. These areas have been selected as being of central importance for a valid comparison.

5 Model answer:

The need for education is crucial in any field. Technology has become critical for economic development, and higher levels of education are constantly demanded by the modern workplace, in both manufacturing and the service sector. Scientific research is clearly related to higher education. The possession of natural resources is no longer so critical for development. Take Japan, a country with few natural riches, where most of the land is mountainous, but which now is one of the world's strongest economies. Effective education, linked with a powerful work ethic and stable government, has allowed Japan to reach this position in a short period of time.

16. Proof-Reading

1a v poverty

1b iv there were

1c   vii   have succeeded
1d   ii   succeed
1e   x   reflects real
1f   vi   registered
1g   i   continents
1h   ix   the German economy
1i   iii   French
1j   viii It can be difficult to decide

2a   *fifty* years
2b   *its* citizens/contribute *to*
2c   *teaches* people knowledge
2d   *whether* it is
2e   There *was*
2f   depends *on/educational* level
2g   the *highest*

3   Note that some flexibility is needed with this exercise. The corrected text below is not perfect English, but is much clearer than the original.

I come from China, which is a very traditional country. I think before *giving* my own situation and *plans*, I have to say something about my country, because *its culture has affected* me very much. My country has 5,000 years *of* history, so in my brain there are a lot of *things* which *are* from it.

When I first arrived *in the* UK I studied in Cambridge, which is the best university *in* the world. Although I just studied in a language school in Cambridge, I felt *very* good. I learned a lot, not only from the school, but also from Cambridge society. That is why I *chose* Cambridge to *study* my foundation course. The foundation course *was* just for *overseas students* to improve their English.

I would like to study *business*, because when China *joins the* WTO, my country will need a lot of people who know business very well. So I will choose *a* business foundation course, *with computing* and mathematics, because *computers are* very useful in modern society. *On* the future course I think the biggest problem *will be* vocabulary, so I am planning to remember as *much* as I can. I will spend more time on mathematics, because I *have* never *studied* it before.

Another problem is to finish homework in time. Sometimes I think homework is *not* useful for me, so I just leave it, which is a bad *custom*. The last and the *greatest problem* is *homesickness*, which always *slows* down my progress, but studying *abroad* is my own choice, *so* I have to try my best.

Part 2: Elements of Writing

1. **Cause and Effect**

   3a   leads to/results in
   3b   Because of/Owing to/Due to
   3c   leads to/causes/results in/produces
   3d   therefore/consequently/which is why
   3e   leads to/causes/results in

   4a   because of/due to/owing to
   4b   because/since
   4c   consequently/therefore
   4d   due to/owing to/because of
   4e   because of/due to/owing to
   4f   so/therefore/thus/consequently

   5   Model answer:

   This results in people having more money to spend, and so leads to higher spending on goods and services. The increased demand for goods and services results in lower unemployment, and consequently the government has a higher income because it spends less on social security.

2. **Cohesion**

   2   they
        this
        the former
        the latter
        these

   3   villagers
        kerosene and diesel
        not being affordable
        villagers'
        kerosene and diesel
        from kerosene and diesel

   4a   They
   4b   he
   4c   them
   4d   This
   4e   his
   4f   he

   5a   It

5Ab her
5Ac She
5Ad him
5Ae They/she
5Af Their
5Ag she
5Ah his

5Ba Their
5Bb their
5Bc They
5Bd their
5Be Their
5Bf the former

3. **Comparisons**

3a slightly more expensive than
3b considerably/significantly cheaper than
3c slightly cheaper than
3d considerably/significantly more expensive than

7a least
7b slightly
7c nearly/almost
7d as
7e most
7f than
7g half
7h as

8a most
8b less
8c more
8d than
8e slightly
8f on
8g as
8h smallest/least

9a shows
9b longest/highest
9c longest
9d On

9e than

9f the

9g slightly

10 Model answer:

The highest rate is found in Greece (8.3 per day), and the lowest is in Norway (1.7). Although many countries are close to the EU average of 4.5, the northern Scandinavian countries all have low rates of smoking.

11. Model answer:

Alcohol consumption in Europe averages 11.1 litres per adult per year, but within this there are wide variations. The highest consumption is found in France (14.1), while the Norwegians only consume one-third of this figure (4.8).

4. **Definitions**

2a instrument/device

2b organs

2c organisation/corporation

2d material

2e behaviour

2f system/process

2g period/time

2h system

3a process   refine liquids

3b person/doctor   mental problems

3c qualification/degree   a dissertation/thesis

3d body/organisation   its members' interests

3e disease   a mosquito-borne parasite

3f cereal/grain   making flour

4a a failed project

4b development

4c electronic commerce

4d attachment

4e self-brightening

Model answers:

5a capital punishment   execution carried out by state, often by hanging

5b department store   large shop that sells most types of goods in different areas

5c   post-natal depression   feeling of sadness experienced by some
                                mothers after birth

5.   **Discussion**

3   Model answer for title (a):

pros: more security for children with mother, mother is able to take
more care of home

cons: children have less chance to mix with others, mothers have
more limited role

Title: Instead of going out to work, mothers should stay at home and
look after their children until they are at least five – Discuss.

a)   Introduction   the growth in women's participation in the
                       work force – increased use of nurseries

b)   Advantages   more social mixing for children

                       higher income for family

                       more varied roles for women

c)   Disadvantages   less security for children

                       women have to deal with career and home

d)   Conclusion   depends on individual situation

4   Model answers:

It has been argued that staying at home gives children security, but
the evidence suggests that there are more social advantages in
attending a nursery.

While fast food is often claimed to be unhealthy, there appears to be
little firm evidence to support this.

6   Model answer:

It appears that Lomborg's definition of air quality is limited to
sulphur dioxide, and fails to take into account more recent threats.

7   Model answer:

pros: concentration of facilities = convenience/availability of high
quality employment, education, health and other services

cons: high costs, noise, pollution, levels of stress, lack of space

8   Model answer using pattern (2ii):

a)   Introduction: definition of city, examples of cities to be used,
     overview of essay

b)   Economic aspects: historical role of industrial cities – relevance in
     post-industrial society?

c)   Social aspects: entertainment, cultural and shopping centres.
     Linked to (b)

d) Discussion/conclusion: changing pattern of city life. Appeal to different ages

6. **Examples**

2a e.g./such as

2b A case in point

2c particularly/especially (*for example/for instance* also possible)

2d for instance/for example

2e such as/e.g.

Model answers:

3a A number of sports such as football/motor racing …

3b Some British universities, for example the University of Leeds …

3c In recent years many women, e.g. Indira Gandhi …

3d … most car makers, for instance Toyota/Volkswagen …

3e Certain diseases, particularly malaria/AIDS …

3f Many musical instruments such as guitars/violins …

3g Several mammals, e.g. pandas/tigers …

4   Customs: holidays and festivals, ways of greeting people
everyday patterns: types of shop, shop opening times
inevitable differences: language, currency
rapid changes of mood: depression, elation
relatively short period: two/three months
some aspects of their new surroundings: freedom, independence

5a His mother's sister, i.e. his aunt …

5b When the liquid reached boiling point, namely 140 degrees …

5c All the plants and animals at risk in the region, that is to say, the endangered wildlife …

5d At this stage, all the students should be rigorously evaluated, viz. given an examination.

5e It was cold, wet and windy, in other words, an English summer's day.

7. **Generalisations**

Model answers:

3b Flowers are usually a suitable present.

3c Cities are often affected by pollution.

3d Fresh fruit can be good for health.

3e Television has become an important medium.

4. Many international students attend British universities. Most welcome the chance to meet classmates from all over the world, and all are pleased to have the chance to improve their English.

5a Unemployment in 1989 was higher than in 1979 or 1999.

5b Inflation was higher in 1979 than in 1989 or 1999.

5c House prices rose dramatically between 1979 and 1989.

5d Interest rates were slightly higher in 1989 than in 1979, and were much lower in 1999.

6a be over 60.

6b double by 2100.

6c young populations/a small proportion of over 60s.

6d fall in its total population/a doubling of the population over 60.

6e have a significant population of older people/a larger proportion of over 60s.

7a Two common dreams are being chased and falling.

7b A majority have dreamed about the dead.

7c Dreaming about the future is quite common.

7d Food dreams may be linked to dieting.

7e A minority dream of finding money.

8. **Numbers**

2a Few people ...

2b They received scores of ...

2c She made various ...

2d He found dozens...

2e They made several ...

Model answers:

4a Three-quarters of the people interviewed said that they supported the president.

4b The average number of students on the course has been 24.

4c The price of petrol has increased eight times/-fold since 1965.

4d Two-thirds of the students in the group were women.

4e The new type of train halved the journey time to Madrid.

4f The majority of the students studied law.

4g There has been a 50% rise in the numbers applying to this department this year.

5b The numbers doubled every year between 1998 and 2000.

5c More than twice as many students complete their first degree course in Britain, compared with Italy.

5d Tap water is much cheaper than bottled water.

5e Only a small percentage/proportion of women believed that they had the same rights as men. Over a third complained that they had far fewer rights.

5f   Life expectancy for men in the UK rose by 50% during the twentieth century.

5g   The cost of the same operation varies by 50% between hospitals in …

5h   The area of forest in England fell by ⅔ between 1086 and 1870.

9. References and Quotations

2   (a), (d) and (e) need references.

5   Model answers:

5a   Orwell (1940) stated that Dickens rarely writes directly about work. He claimed that most of Dickens' characters, except David Copperfield, have shadowy occupations, and that Copperfield works in areas very similar to Dickens' own experience.

5b   Orwell pointed out that Dickens infrequently described his characters' jobs clearly: 'In Dickens' novels anything in the nature of work happens off-stage. The only one of his heroes who has a plausible profession is David Copperfield …' (Orwell, 1940: pp. 54–55)

5c   According to Orwell (1940), few of Dickens' characters have a convincing profession, with the exception of David Copperfield, who follows Dickens' own career. 'With most of the others, the way they earn their living is very much in the background.' (pp. 54–55)

8a   alphabetically

8bi   author/date of publication/title/place of publication/publisher

8bii   author/date of publication/title/editor/main title/place of publication/publisher

8biii   author/title/URL/access date

8biv   author/article title/journal name/issue/page number

8c   book and journal titles

8d   for titles of books (but not articles)

8e   under the title of the publication

10. Academic Style

Model answers:

4a   It is widely believed that the railways are deteriorating.

4b   Serious crime, such as murder, is increasing.

4c   The figures in that report are not reliable.

4d   The second factor is that the majority of children in that district may become criminals.

4e   There appears to be a significant risk of further strikes and disorder.

4f   Women were enfranchised in 1994.

4g   The Russian inflation led to poverty and disease.

4h   A malaria vaccine may be discovered in the next ten years.

4i There were two main causes of the American Revolution.

5a Currently, significant numbers of children are starting school at the age of four or less, whereas thirty years ago five was the normal age. There appear to be various reasons for the change; mothers, for example, need to rejoin the labour force. There are mixed views about the effects of this change on the children concerned. Jenkins (1989) claims that early school attendance causes social problems such as theft and drug taking. There seems to be considerable evidence to support his views and there may be an argument in favour of a state subsidy for women to stay at home with their children.

5b There appear to be two principal reasons for the growing traffic congestion. Firstly, public transport has become increasingly expensive relative to the falling cost of motoring. In addition, car ownership is much more convenient than using public transport. Together, these factors result in higher vehicle density.

11. Synonyms

Model answers:

4a challenged/outcome/study

4b data or figures/demonstrate/increase

4c forecast/argument or debate

4d main disadvantage/method

4e focus/possibility

4f explain/idea or theory

4g topics/evaluated

4h structure/kept/targets/changed

4i reduce output/increase

4j tendency/accelerated

5 firm's plan
cut expenditure or spending
leading executives or managers
salaries or earnings reduced
intends
salaries or earnings
raised

6 UK – British – this country
agency – organisation – body
advertising campaign – publicity programme – advertising blitz
to raise – to improve
British eating habits – regular hand washing
to cut – reduction

12. **Visual Information**

1.1 dE

1.2 fB

1.3 aF

1.4 cC

1.5 bD

1.6 eA

Model answers:

2a grew slightly

2b rose steadily

2c fell sharply

2d increased slightly

2e sharp rise

2f slight drop

3   (a) is better because it selects the most important details. (b) simply repeats the data on the chart.

Model answers:

4a density

4b illustrates/shows

4c between

4d emptier/less-crowded

4e role/part

4f since/because

4g tend

5a table

5b range/variety

5c marriage

5d Britain

5e rate

5f Iran

5g half

5h proportion/figure

5i result/consequence

7   Model answer:

Table 4 shows the gender balance in the School of Computing from 1996 to 2000. Between 1996 and 1998 the ratio of men to women was about 1:3, but in the next two years the proportion of women increased, so that in 2000 women accounted for nearly 40% of the total.

Part 3: Accuracy in Writing

1.   Abbreviations

10a Prime Minister/Members of Parliament/National Health Service

10b Information Technology/and others

10c That is/World Trade Organisation

10d Take note/Curricula vitaea/A4 size paper

10e Organisation for Economic Co-operation and Development/United Kingdom

10f European Union/Value Added Tax

10g Chief Executive Officer/Research and development

10h Figure 4/World wide web

10i World Health Organisation/tuberculosis

10j Public Relations/$45,000

10k Genetically modified/for example

10l Professor/Master of Philosophy/Doctor of Philosophy

2.   Adverbs

4a Obviously/Clearly

4b Originally

4c Alternatively

4d Recently/Lately

4e Similarly

4f Clearly/Obviously

5   Time: gradually/slowly/steadily/rapidly/quickly
    Amount: slightly/marginally/substantially/significantly/considerably/sharply/dramatically

(Others may be acceptable.)

6a slightly

6b substantially/significantly

6c dramatically

6d steadily

6e considerably/substantially/significantly

6f rapidly/quickly

6g slowly/slightly

6h rapidly

3. **Articles**

    4a –

    4b –

    4c The/the

    4d –/the

    4e –/the

    4f The/the

    5a The/the

    5b the/–

    5c The/–/–

    5d the/the

    5e The/the

    6a a

    6b –

    6c the

    6d the

    6e the/a

    6f the

    6g the

    6h a

    6i the

    6j the

    6k the

    6l a

    6m a

    6n The

    6o the

    6p –

    6q The

    6r the

    6s the/a

    6t the

    6u the

    6v the

    6w the

    6x a

    6y the

4. **Caution**

2. These are suggestions. Others are possible.

Modals:	might/may/could/should
Adverbs:	often/usually/frequently/generally/ occasionally/rarely/mainly
Phrases:	in general/by and large/it appears/it seems

3. Model answers:

3a Private companies tend to be …

3b Computer manuals can be …

3c Older students frequently perform better …

3d Exploring space could be …

3e English pronunciation is often …

3f Global warming may cause …

3g Science students tend to work harder …

3h Concrete is usually …

5   Model answer:

A team of American scientists *may* have found a way to reverse the ageing process. They fed diet supplements, *usually* found in health food shops, to elderly rats, which were then tested for memory and stamina. The animals *tended to* display more active behaviour after taking the supplements, and *generally* their memory improved. In addition, their appearance became *rather* more youthful and their appetite increased.

The researchers *believe* that this experiment is *quite* a clear indication of how the problems of old age *may* be overcome. They *claim* that in a few years' time *many people may* be able to look forward to a *fairly* long and active retirement.

5. **Conjunctions**

2a d

2b c

2c f

2d e

2e a

2f b

2g b

2h e

3   Some suggestions (others are possible):
    Addition: moreover/as well as/in addition/and/also
    Result: therefore/consequently/so/that is why
    Reason: because/as a result of/as/since

Time: after/while/then/next/subsequently

Example: such as/e.g./in particular

Opposition: but/yet/while/however/nevertheless/whereas

(Other answers possible.)

4a Because/since

4b i.e./namely

4c After

4d Although/While

4e moreover/furthermore

4f so/therefore

5a After

5b Despite/In spite of

5c such as

5d In addition/Furthermore

5e then/later

5f while

5g Because of/Owing to

5h although/though

5i since/because/as

5j and

5k However

5l so

5m finally

6a While the government claimed that inflation was falling, the opposition said it was rising.

Despite the fact that the government claimed (that) inflation was falling, the opposition …

6b This department must reduce expenditure, but it needs to install new computers.

Although this department must reduce expenditure, it needs …

Model answers:

7a In contrast to America, where gun ownership is common, guns are rare in Japan.

7b Despite leaving school at the age of 14 he went on to own a chain of shops.

7c The majority displayed a positive attitude to the proposal, but a minority rejected it.

7d The review has examined six studies of medical policy; however, none was found relevant to our needs.

7e Although the spring was cold and dry, the summer was warm and wet.

6. **Formality in Verbs**

2 Possible synonyms:
   adapt = modify
   arise = occur
   carry out = conduct
   characterise = have features of
   clarify = explain
   concentrate on = look at closely
   be concerned with = deal with
   demonstrate = show
   determine = find
   discriminate = distinguish
   emphasise = highlight
   establish = lay down/found
   exhibit = show
   focus on = look at closely
   generate = create
   hold = be true
   identify = pick out
   imply = suggest
   indicate = show
   interact = work together
   interpret = explain
   manifest = show
   overcome = get over
   predict = forecast
   propose = suggest
   prove = turn out
   recognise = accept
   relate to = link to
   supplement = add to
   undergo = experience
   yield = produce

3a yielded
3b arose
3c demonstrate
3d held
3e emphasised
3f exhibited

3g concerned

3h carried out

4a demonstrate

4b clarify

4c recognised

4d discriminate

4e predict

4f focus on

4g interpreted

4h overcome

7. **Modal Verbs**

(Others may be possible throughout this unit.)

2a can

2b could

2c cannot

2d may/can

2e could

3a would

3b might/may/could

3c could/might/may

3d should/will/might

3e will

3f should/will

4a should

4b must

4c must

4d should

5a would (conditional)
    should (suggestion)

5b may (possibility)
    could (ability)

5c will (prediction)
    would (conditional)

5d must (obligation)
    should (suggestion)

5e may (possibility)
    could (ability)

5f should (strong possibility)
    may (possibility)

8.   **Nationality Language**

3   Model answer:
    Mexico is in central America.
    The Mexican capital is Mexico City.
    Mexicans speak Spanish.

5a   Chinese
5b   Russian
5c   Australia
5d   Spanish
5e   South African
5f   Brazilians
5g   Iraqi
5h   Cubans

6   Model answers:
    Bill Clinton is an American ex-president.
    Pablo Picasso came from Spain.
    Bob Marley was a Jamaican musician.

9.   **Nouns and Adjectives**

2a   safety – safe
2b   culture – cultural
2c   deep – depth
2d   health – healthy

3   high/reliable/hot
    strength/confidence/truth
    wide/probable/necessary
    length/danger/relevance

4a   unreliable
4b   truth
4c   probability
4d   wide
4e   necessary
4f   relevance
4g   danger
4h   necessity
4i   strength
4j   Confidence

5a   various – variety

5b   analytical – analysis

5c   available – availability

5d   major – majority

5e   precise – precision/unknown – knowledge

5f   theoretical – theory

5g   frequent – frequency

5h   critical – criticism or critic

5i   Social – society

5j   practical – practice

6   particularity
     superior/reasonable
     strategy/synthesis
     political/economic + economical
     industry/culture
     external/average

7a   economic
     approximation
     particularity
     external
     synthesis
     average
     reasonable
     culture

10. Countable and Uncountable Nouns

3   Model answers:

3a   … of teaching is required

3b   … travelling in the desert

3c   … insufficient capital

3d   … during a meal

3e   … mainly political centres

3f   … are moved around the world daily

3g   … huge loss of life

3h   … many great films

3i   Her carelessness …

3j   … a great leveller

3k … in those laboratories

3l … very demanding

5a Little

5b businesses

5c experience/is

5d travel broadens

5e Paper was

5f much advice

5g few interests

5h war

5i Irons were

5j behaviour

6a little

6b much

6c many

6d few

6e little

11. Passives

2a The data was collected and the two groups (were) compared.

2b 120 people in three social classes were interviewed.

2c The results were checked and several errors (were) found.

3a 40% of the houses in the port were badly damaged by a storm.

3b The company was efficiently run by the Connors family until 1981.

3c The house was conveniently built near the station.

3d The portrait of the old man was brilliantly painted by Picasso.

3e Pencils for all the students in the exam were helpfully provided.

3f Over 550 people were regularly tested for the disease (by doctors) over a three-year period.

3g The percentages were precisely calculated to three decimal places (by researchers).

3h Their business was optimistically called the Universal Trading Company.

4 Passives

was worn out

was born

was called

was helped

was taken over

was assisted

5   not all – *was born* must be passive

Compare some sentences changed into the active, e.g. 'On his death in 1860 his wife took over the business, and soon their 10 year-old son Jesse assisted her.' This reads rather clumsily compared with the original.

6   Suggested changes (others possible):

they were married – they married

the factories were used to make – the factories made

Boots was sold – he sold Boots

Boots was bought by a British group – a British group bought Boots

sugar was produced – the factories produced

12. Prefixes and Suffixes

3

auto	by itself
co	together
ex	(i) previous
	(ii) outside
micro	small
multi	many
over	too much
post	later
re	again
sub	below
under	(i) below
	(ii) not enough

4a   social class at bottom of society

4b   more tickets sold than seats available

4c   very local climate

4d   economy based on information not production

4e   not listed in the telephone book

4f   part of the mind not fully conscious

8a   noun – something that is no longer offered

8b   adjective – not able to be forecast

8c   adjective – two related events at the same time

8d   adjective – able to be sold

8e   adverb – without cooperation

8f   noun – person being interviewed

8g   adjective – related to evolution

8h   noun – style of ultra-realistic painting

8i   noun – person who protests

8j   adverb – in a way that suggests a symbol

9a   joint production/junior company

9b   without choosing to/not hurt

9c   able to be refilled/certain

9d   cannot be provided/unusual

9e   existing in theory/breaking into pieces

13. Prepositions

1.   purpose *of*/development *of*/*in* Britain/*over* the period/contributed *to*/valuable *for*/*In* conclusion/sets *out*/relationship *between*/decline *in*/supply *of*/*in* the factory

Verb + = contributed to

Adj + = valuable for

Phrasal verb = sets out

Place = in Britain/factory

Time = over the period

Phrase = In conclusion

2b   adjective +

2c   verb +

2d   prep. place

2e   noun +

2f   phrase

2g   prep. place

2h   prep. time

3a   of

3b   in

3c   of

3d   of

3e   on

4a   On

4b   of

4c   of

4d   In

4e   of

5a Among

5b from/to

5c in/of

5d in/in

5e in/at

5f On/between

6a out

6b of

6c in/to

6d to

6e among/in

6f from

6g between

6h in

6i of

6j over

6k between

6l in

6m in

6n of

6o in/to

14. Prepositions after Verbs

2a focused on/concentrated on

2b pointed out

2c specialising in

2d associated with

2e divided into

2f blamed for

2g believed in

2h rely on

4a derives from

4b consists of

4c added to

4d looked into

4e rely on/depend on

4f invested … in

4g Compared with

4h   pay ... for

4i   rely on/depend on

15. Punctuation

7a   On Tuesday June 6, 1759, in the church at Derby, Nicolas James married Mary Dewey.

7b   Professor Rowan's new book, *The Triumph of Capitalism*, is published in New York.

7c   How many people would agree with John Lennon when he said: 'All you Need is Love'?

7d   The probability was calculated for each of the three faculties: Physics, Biology and Law.

7e   As Cammack (1994) points out: 'Latin America is creating a new phenomenon: democracy without citizens.'

7f   Thousands of new words such as 'website' enter the English language each year.

7g   Dr Tanner's latest study focuses on children's reactions to stress in the playground.

7h   She scored 56% on the main course; the previous semester she had achieved 67%.

8   The London School of Business is offering three new courses this year: Economics with Psychology; Introduction to Management; and e-commerce. The first is taught by Dr Jennifer Hillary and runs from October to January. The second, Introduction to Management, for MSc. Finance students is offered in the second semester, and is assessed by coursework only. Professor Wang's course in e-commerce runs in both the autumn and the spring, and is for more experienced students.

16. Referring Verbs

(Others may be possible.)

3a   A admitted/accepted/agreed that he might have made a mistake in his estimate.

3b   B denied saying that sheep were faster than horses.

3c   C stated that whales were very intelligent animals.

3d   D agreed with A's position on cats and dogs.

3e   E assumed that cows could get cold in winter.

3f   F concluded that pigs could not fly.

3g   G discovered a new type of frog in the jungle.

3h   H doubted that cats could learn to talk.

3i   I suggested that cat and mouse behaviour should be compared.

3j   J hypothesised that there might be a link between health and the seasons.

5a K blamed X's work for a lot of our current problems.

5b L criticised her for being careless about her research methods.

5c M classified bees into three main species.

5d N characterised the cat family as the kings of the animal world.

5e O interpreted dogs' barking as nervousness.

5f P described trying to estimate the number of animal species as being like shooting in the dark.

5g Q evaluated Darwin as the greatest naturalist of the nineteenth century.

5h R defined insects as six-legged arthropods.

5i S portrayed Queen Victoria as a short, rather fat, dark-eyed woman.

5j T identified/presented Gregor Mendel as the founder of modern genetics.

17. Relative Pronouns

1a where

1b who

1c which/that

1d whose

2a which/that

2b where

2c who

2d which/that

2e who

2f which

4a D

4b D

4c A

4d A

4e D

5a necessary

5b not

5c not

5d necessary

5e not

6a whose

6b who

6c which/that

6d which/that

6e x
6f which
6g whose
6h which
6i x

18. **Singular/Plural**

1a disadvantages – e
1b are – a
1c areas – c
1d crime – b
1e town has its own council – d

3a those problems
3b colleges
3c varies
3d cultures
3e are
3f a job/jobs
3g A huge/huge numbers
3h has
3i other places
3j is
3k lives

4 companies have/websites/e-commerce/this is/businesses/their/
trouble/security/expense/mean/these companies

19. **Tenses**

1

	Tense	Reason for use
a	present simple	general rule
b	present continuous	current situation
c	present perfect	recent event
d	present perfect continuous	recent, with emphasis on action that continues for a long time
e	simple past	finished, with time phrase
f	past continuous	finished, with emphasis on action that continues for a long time
g	past perfect	refers to a previous past period
h	*will* future	prediction

(Others may be possible.)

2a   has been rising

2b   stands for

2c   recorded

2d   had written

2e   will be

2f   is considering

2g   was building/had built

2h   disputes/disputed

2i   has fallen/has been falling

4a   is working

4b   believes

4c   is looking for

4d   is researching

4e   has risen

4f   owns

4g   live

4h   is attending

6a   have suspected

6b   have developed

6c   confirmed

6d   developed

6e   was displayed

6f   demonstrated

6g   says/said

6h   is being tested

6i   makes

6j   developed

6k   will be available

20. **Time Words and Phrases**

3a   Last

3b   During

3c   By

3d   for

3e   ago

3f   until

3g   Currently

4a   recently
4b   until
4c   for
4d   Last month
4e   by
4f   Since
4g   During

5a   During
5b   Since
5c   ago
5d   recently
5e   Currently
5f   by
5g   since

6a   before
6b   later
6c   by
6d   for
6e   until
6f   during
6g   ago

Part 4: Writing Models

1. **Formal Letters**

   1a   Address of sender

   1b   Address of recipient

   1c   Sender's reference

   1d   Date

   1e   Greeting

   1f   Subject headline

   1g   Reason for writing

   1h   Further details

   1i   Request for response

   1j   Ending

   1k   Signature

   1l   Writer's name and title

   2   Model answer:

---

54 Sydney Road
Rowborough
RB1 6FD

Mr M Bramble

Administrative Assistant

Arts & Social Sciences Admissions Office

Wye House

Central Campus

University of Borchester

Borchester BR3 5HT

Yr Ref.: MB/373

5 May 2002

Dear Mr Bramble

Informal Interview

Thank you for inviting me to interview on May 21st. I will be able to attend on that date, but it would be much more convenient if I could have the interview at 12, due to the train times from Rowborough.

Could you please let me know if this alteration is possible?

Yours sincerely

P. Tan

P. Tan

---

3 Model answer:

54 Sydney Road
Rowborough
RB1 6FD
Tel: 0122-354-751

The Manager
Hotel Nelson
Queen's Road
Rowborough RB2 4RN

Yr Ref.: EN2

16 October 2002

Dear Sir

Vacancy for Reception Staff

I am writing in response to your advert for reception staff (*Evening News* 15/10).

I am currently studying at Rowborough University, but I am looking for part-time work, and believe that I have the qualities you are seeking. As you will see from my enclosed CV I have previous experience of working in a team, and speak Mandarin and Japanese as well as English. Having no family commitments I am quite prepared to work evenings or weekends.

I believe that I could make a useful contribution to your business, which I am considering as a future career, and hope to hear from you soon.

Yours faithfully

P. Tan

P. Tan

Enc. CV

3. Designing and Reporting Surveys

1 (Other suggestions possible/in any order.)

Get up-to-date data

Collect information about the behaviour of a specific group, e.g. overseas students in London

Check/replicate other research

2a conducted

2b random

2c questionnaire

2d questioned

2e respondents

2f Interviewees

2g mentioned

2h majority

2i slightly

2j minority

2k questions

2l common

2m generally

2n sample

3   Model questions (Q3–Q6 could use present tense):

Q2 Why did you take a job?

Q3 What effect did the work have on your studies?

Q4 What kind of work did you do?

Q5 What hours did you work?

Q6 How much did you earn?

Q7 Do you have any comments on your work?

4a past tense

4b present tense

The survey is completed but the results are still valid.

5   (ii) is less embarrassing for most people to answer.

6   (i) is an open question and has many possible answers.

(ii) is a closed question with a limited range of responses.

4. **Comparison Essay**

(Other answers possible.)

a   This normally involves having access to a secure site on the internet where a graded series of lessons is available, which have assignments sent and returned by email.

b   A student living in a small town in China, for example, can now study a course at an American college.

c   Membership of a group may also create a useful spirit of competition which stimulates learning.

d   There may be many people who are unable, through either work or family commitments, or owing to lack of funds, to go to classes …

e   Although online courses are now offered by many institutions …

f   … it is by no means clear that they offer real advantages compared with classroom education.

g   e-education/online courses/internet use in education/e-learning

5 **Discursive Essay**
   1   Definition 1 (national development)
   2   Reason
   3   Example
   4   Definition 2 (education)
   5   Topic
   6   Outline

Writing Tests

Writing Test 1
SPEAKING AND WRITING
1)   When we speak, it is normally to one or
2)   a small number of people, who are often well known to us.
3)   As we speak, we are able
4)   to study our listeners' faces for expressions that tell
5)   us their reaction to what we are saying;
6)   for example agreement, or amusement.
7)   If their expressions show incomprehension
8)   we will probably restate what we are saying.
9)   For most people speaking feels like a natural activity,
10) though if they have to make a formal speech
11) they often find the situation stressful.

1)   Writing, however, is much more like speaking to
2)   an unknown audience.
3)   Unless we are writing a letter to a friend
4)   we have no way of knowing who may read our words.
5)   Writers cannot check if the readers understand, or are interested
6)   in what they are writing.
7)   This is the reason why writing is more difficult than
8)   speaking, and often uses a more formal style.
9)   It also explains why writing must be as clear and simple as possible,
10) to avoid the dangers of being misunderstood by readers,
11) who cannot look puzzled to
12) make the writer explain what he means again.

Writing Test 2
   Note that in some cases, e.g. (1a), only one answer is acceptable; in
   other cases, e.g. (1b), a number of synonyms are possible, not all of
   which may be listed.

1a   in

1b   problem/difficulty/challenge/priority

1c   the/so

1d   difficult/problematic/challenging

1e   However/Next/Then

1f   or

1g   improves

1h   begins/tends/seems

1i   in/after

1j   they

1k   easily/well/effectively

1l   third/further

1m   most

1n   since/because/as

1o   on

1p   why

1q   necessary/better/useful/helpful

1r   an

1s   before

1t   their

Writing Test 3

Note comments in Writing Test 1 above.

3a   somewhere

3b   from

3c   who

3d   kinds/types/sorts/categories

3e   Almost/Nearly/Virtually

3f   halls

3g   make/find

3h   convenient/practical/sensible

3i   but/although/though

3j   rather

3k   a

3l   This

3m   may/might/can/could/should

3n   also

3o   on

3p as/since/because

3q be

3r vital/important/essential/critical

3s an

3t them

Writing Test 4

Model answer:

A COMPARISON OF BORCHESTER AND ROWBOROUGH AS A STUDY LOCATION

Rowborough is a large industrial city with a population of one and a half million, whereas Borchester is an old city with a much smaller population. These basic differences determine their suitability as centres for a university course.

Rowborough can offer a wider range of leisure facilities but Borchester has a quieter character. Rowborough may have a worse climate, being cool even in summer and wet in winter, while winters in Borchester are less cold, though the summers tend to be wet.

Rowborough is hillier than Borchester, which might be a drawback for cyclists. However, Rowborough does have a better public transport system, which may compensate for the hills. Borchester also has a rather remote campus, which might involve a lot of travelling. It is also likely to be more expensive in terms of accommodation, and is rather distant from the capital. On the other hand, some areas in Rowborough suffer from high crime rates.

Clearly, each city has its advantages: Borchester is more likely to suit a student looking for peace and quiet, who can tolerate some inconvenience, while Rowborough would be suitable for someone keen to economise and wanting a more lively atmosphere.

Sources

Quotations from the following articles will be found in various units. As the quotations have been made to give examples of language, rather than for reasons of content, in-text references are not made.

Ardila, A. 2001. Predictors of university academic performance in Colombia. *International Journal of Educational Research* 35 (4): 411–417

Bardet, J.-P. 2001. Early marriage in pre-modern France. *The History of the Family* 6 (3) 345–363

Benoit, D., Madigan, S., Lecce, S., Shea, B. and Goldberg, S. 2001. Atypical maternal behaviour toward feeding-disordered infants before and after intervention. *Infant Mental Health Journal* 22 (6): 611–626

Chakrabarti, S. and Chakrabarti, S. Rural electrification programme with solar energy in remote region – a case study in an island. *Energy Policy* 30 (1): 33–42

Creeber, G. 2001. 'Taking our personal lives seriously': intimacy, continuity and memory in the television serial. *Media, Culture & Society* 23: 439–455

Davis, G. 2002. Is the claim that 'variance kills' an ecological fallacy? *Accident Analysis and Prevention* 34 (3): 343–346

Dündar, Ö. 2001. Models of urban transformation. Informal housing in Ankara. *Cities* 18 (6): 391–401

Grant, J., Meller, W. and Urevig, B. 2001. Changes in psychiatric consultations over ten years. *General Hospital Psychiatry* 23 (5): 261–265

Hendry, E. 2001. Masonry walls: materials and constructions. *Construction and Building Materials* 15 (8): 323–330

Horton, E., Folland, C. and Parker, D. 2001. The changing incidence of extremes in worldwide and central England temperatures to the end of the twentieth century. *Climatic Change* 50: 267–295

Job, N., van Exel, A. and Rietveld, P. 2001. Public transport strikes and traveller behaviour. *Transport Policy* 8 (4): 237–246

Kinder, T. 2001. The use of call centres by local public administrations. *Futures* 33 (10): 837–860

Marxsen, C. 2001. Potential world garbage and waste carbon sequestration. *Environmental Science & Policy* 4 (6): 293–300

Nazarov, V., Radostin, A. and Stepanyants, Y. 2001. Influence of water content in river sand on the self-brightening of acoustic waves. *Applied Acoustics* 62 (12): 1347–1358

O'Sullivan, D. 2002. Framework for managing business development in the networked organisation. *Computers in Industry* 47 (1): 77–88

Otero, J. and Milas, C. 2001. Modelling the spot prices of various coffee types. *Economic Modelling* 18 (4): 625–641

Pogrebin, M. and Dodge, M. 2001. Women's accounts of their prison experiences. A retrospective view of their subjective realities. *Journal of Criminal Justice* 29 (6): 531–541

Sánchez–Moreno, E. 2001. Cross-cultural links in ancient Iberia: socio-economic anatomy of hospitality. *Oxford Journal of Archaeology* 20 (4): 391–414

Selmer, J. 2001. Coping and adjustment of Western expatriate managers in Hong Kong. *Scandinavian Journal of Management* 17 (2): 167–185

Semple, J. 2000. Production of transgenic rice with agronomically useful genes. *Biotechnology Advances* 18 (8): 653–683

Smith, L. and Haddad, L. 2001. How important is improving food availability for reducing child nutrition in developing countries? *Agricultural Economics* 26 (3): 191–204

Tedesco, L. 2000. La nãta contra el vidrio: urban violence and democratic governability in Argentina. *Bulletin of Latin American Research* 19 (4): 527–545

Worthington, R. 2001. Between Hermes and Themis: an empirical study of the contemporary judiciary in Singapore. *Journal of Law & Society* 28 (4): 490–519